MADE TO CHANGE THE WORLD

Your Life Matters

COACH BRIAN WILLIAMS

Foreword by
TOM ZIGLAR

Inspired for Life Media, Florida

Made to Change the World - Your Life Matters

Published by: Inspired for Life Media, Florida

Proofread by Dale Williams

Manuscript review by Lisa Easterling and Kathy Swigle

Design by Tyler Flores

Printed and bound in the United States of America

Visit us on the web at madetochangetheworld.com

GET YOUR CERTIFICATE

I will send you a completion certificate after you read
Made to Change the World
By Coach Brian Williams

Become a World Changer for Christ!

After you read the book and post your review on Amazon, click this link to get your completion certificate. www. madetochangetheworld.com / certificate

You can collect all MTCTW certificates by completing:

- Made to Change the World book
- Made to Change the World Small Group Study
- Made to Change the World Small Group Leader
- Made to Change the World Monthly Member
- Made to Change the World Coach Training
- Made to Change the World Pastor/Ministry Leader

ABOUT THE AUTHOR

Brian Williams is a double Board-Certified Coach and a Professional Certified Coach (PCC) through the International Coaching Federation. He has coached thousands of people and has led a staff of coaches whose combined efforts have positively impacted the lives of hundreds of thousands.

Brian has extensive experience in helping people improve key areas of their lives including wellness, career, business, relationships, and most importantly, walking with Jesus. He has helped them fulfill their God-ordained purpose through the direction of Jesus Christ. He partners with each person to help him or her clearly move forward by taking the right steps, and, through accountability and encouragement, to achieve those goals.

Brian is also an ordained pastor through the Anchor Bay Evangelistic Association. He uses his spiritual background and training to help others grow through coaching, and has helped lead prayer ministries, facilitate small groups, and organize various spiritual campaigns and church projects. Brian, along with his wife Claudia and their daughter Ellie, attend and serve at FishHawk Fellowship Church in Lithia, Florida.

f

BOOKS BY COACH BRIAN WILLIAMS:

Made to Change the World - Your Life Matters

This book will encourage you to know God's calling then provide the tools to live it in every area of your life with an impact that will change the world around you.

Made to Change the World - Your Life Matters, Small Group Study

This six-week study not only walks your group through how to understand God's calling but also provides the way to change and live it out.

Walk With God Today

Grow closer to God through this daily devotional that will not only challenge you to think deeper in your faith but to make the changes in your life in order to walk closer with God each day.

Directions for Life

If you want to know the purpose, mission and vision God has for your life and also live it, this is the book for you. This is the starting point to following the call God has for you each day of your life.

Talk Truth to Yourself

We easily get off track in life because we believe things that are not true about God and His promises. This book will teach how to know and to live the truth to receive God's promises.

Life Wise: How to Live by God's Wisdom

One book of the Bible clearly talks about how to be successful, God's way, in every area of life. This book will not only explore what God says but also show how to live it out.

Having Balance in Life As a Christian

Balanced living in God's eyes isn't the same as what the world considers to be as balance. More importantly than us figuring out how to balance our own lives, it is surrendering each area to God.

Theology of Behavior Change

Many Christians want to change areas in their life or follow God more closely in faith but do not know how to make changes that last. This book explains how to change and gives supporting tools.

For all of these books as well as additional resources to help you fully live the life God desires for you and impact the world around you, go to: www. madetochangetheworld.com/resources. Make sure to watch the short video on our home page and to register to get free weekly emails with videos, tools, and encouragement to support you in your walk with God.

Pastors and Ministry Leaders – See "Pastors and Ministry Leaders" tab at our website www.madetochangetheworld.com/pastors for tools to help you disciple those you lead.

FOREWORD BY TOM ZIGLAR

Made to Change the World: Your Life Matters, is a powerful book. Let me prove it to you.

Say this to yourself right now: "I am made to change the world. My life matters." Let it sink in. How does it feel? Do you know it's true? Do you wish it were true?

Good news. YOU ARE made to change the world. But how? That is what this book reveals. Now say it again - move your lips this time! "**I Am** made to change the world. My life matters."

Do you realize what you just did? You used God's name, "I Am" to proclaim your purpose. To change the world - to matter. Now that is powerful! But how? It starts with surrender. You are made to change the world and that takes a lot of resources. The resources inside you are limited. You only have so much. But that is okay. God is unlimited and He is ready to fill you and supply every need you have. Imagine a pipeline of love, grace, and resources flowing from God to you. The only challenge is that the flow is a trickle and you are constantly depleting your own resources. And yet you have an unlimited supply if you could only...and then you see it. There is a valve on the pipeline between you and God. On the valve is the word *Surrender.* Suddenly, you turn the knob and you are overwhelmed with God's goodness!

Dig into this book and you will discover how you can surrender and be overwhelmed with God's goodness in every area of your life. You are made to change the world! It's time to get started!

Tom Ziglar

CEO of Zig Ziglar

PREFACE

IMPORTANT!

The book you are about to read can be informational or literally trans-
formational! It is really up to you and based on how you want to use it.
At a minimum, this book will get you thinking about the importance of
your life, your walk with God, and how you live today in light of eternity. It will cause you to think about how you are living and thinking,
and whether or not you are having the greatest adventure and fulfilled
life Jesus Christ has planned for you.

At its most effective level, this book will cause you to look deep into
the core of who you are and who God is, and it will change and transform your thinking and your life as you walk day by day, step by step,
and moment by moment. This will lead you to the greatest adventure
of your life and also an eternity with many others whom you have
impacted and touched along the way for the sake of Jesus Christ.

My background of helping well over a thousand people through
hands-on coaching, mentoring, and teaching has prepared me for the
writing of this book. I personally have made big shifts and changes in
my life and thinking as I have been led by God, and because of this,
have the opportunity to help a great number of others change their

lives as well. Through all this I realized that we are all exactly the same – at the core of each of us is the desire to be loved, to know God, and to fulfill his purpose. Unfortunately, many people--including Christians--don't live or experience these things fully in their own lives. I am here to say that you can, and you will if you are steadfast in your pursuit of God and His purpose for your life. I have provided some help and support through this book to lead you to achieve just that.

It is important to understand that living fully for Christ does not mean your life will be free of challenges, obstacles, or even very difficult situations. It does mean that you will have success (the way God defines it), complete fulfillment, incredible adventure, and the greatest news of all, the opportunity at the end of your life to hear your Lord and Father, the creator of you and all the universe say, "Well done good and faithful servant!"

I believe that if you live a life fully devoted to God by knowing Him, following Him and living according to His purpose, He will use you in mighty ways. Your life will not only be fulfilling for you, but will change the world by impacting the people around you.

HOW TO USE THIS BOOK

Through the process of writing *Made to Change the World,* many other tools, books, and resources were developed. The original book idea morphed into a full life change program. Depending on the level that you want to be involved and walk closer with God, there are tools to help you do it. The goal of this book and all that goes with it is not just to help you learn something new and get excited about life. The goal is to literally help you change who you are, in every area of life, to fully live for God so that you may receive all His promises and fulfill His purpose. In the process, you will change the world around you.

This book is designed and recommended to be used with the small group study or at minimum a person who can partner with you through it. Below is a description of how to use, absorb, and put into practice what you read. I challenge you to not only read this book but to live it. To get the maximum use out of the *Made to Change the World* book and program, do these things as you get ready to start the book.

Step 1 – Go to www.madetochangetheworld.com to register for free weekly emails that contain videos, tools, and support to help you grow and change.

Step 2 - Consider using *Made to Change the World Small Group Study* to partner and grow with others. Working together through learning and growth is the very best way to make lasting change.

Step 3 – Look into additional books, tools, and support provided through the *Made to Change the World* program. These options include memberships, workbooks, and Christian Coaching.

It is also important to note that this book is not designed to teach you to fly solo in life. It is designed to help you grow in your relationships with others and to encourage you to ask others to walk with you through these changes. As the Bible says, "man sharpens man like iron sharpens iron", which applies equally to men and women. A word of caution here: it is highly recommended that you have a same-sex accountability partner unless, of course, that person is your spouse or another family member.

Take *Made to Change the World* as a challenge to not only change your own life, but the lives of those around you by fully living your purpose. Jesus said that we would do greater works than He did, so here is a very important question to consider: why aren't we each doing these greater works right now? Consider that question as you read and realize that your life matters. You were made to change the world!

DO YOU KNOW JESUS?

This book will be a great help for your walk with Jesus. However, I realize some of you reading this may not know what it means to be a Christian or even if you are one. This section is for you and will help you not only understand what being a Christian means but also help you make the most important decision in your life if you are ready.

I will start with my background and how I became a Christian. In my early 20s, I graduated from college and moved to Florida. Even though I was already becoming successful at a young age, I found myself on Clearwater Beach one Saturday in a miserable state of mind. Even though I had grown up going to church, I ended up hopeless and all the accomplishments, friends, church sermons, and other things I had in life did not bring fulfillment. I asked myself what the purpose was in continuing to move forward in life.

When I got to my lowest low and sat on the beach that day, I looked around at the sky, the ocean, and the birds flying, and realized that no man made what I saw and no man controls it. I knew I couldn't make it on my own and needed a bigger purpose and reason for life. I also knew what it meant to turn my life over to God, so I prayed to Jesus and surrendered my life to Him. I knew that I had sinned (missed the mark) many times in my life and asked Jesus to forgive me. I asked Jesus to give me His purpose and direction. I committed to pray and read the Bible every day and promised God that if He would help me out of my miserable mess, I would tell everyone I could about His love and forgiveness and about the transformation in my life. So here I am writing this to you because of this complete transformation of my life.

I have kept that commitment to spend daily time with Him each morning over the past 20 years. I can probably count on one hand the number of times I have missed praying and Bible reading. There were some big changes God walked me through over the months and years that followed my day at the beach, including putting away my selfish desires and changing my focus and thinking in order to believe what is true based on what He says in the Bible. He empowers me to pursue a much bigger and more important purpose for my life here on earth and for eternity.

I have talked with many people and it is easy to see that what the Bible says is true – we all are in the same boat of having sinned in our lives. Sin is the opposite of God's will and is mainly formed from our selfish desires and attitudes. Sin includes things like anger, jealousy, bitterness, fear, unbelieving, immoral thoughts, sexuality outside of marriage, lying, wanting someone else's property, and lust, just to name a few. It is putting yourself and "things" in life as the most important in the place of God. Sin is disobedience to God and not living the way he wants us to live which is to work together here on this earth through His love.

God has a plan for you not only here on earth, but also for eternity. The problem is that sin separates us from God and causes a chasm between us. This is a chasm we cannot cross on our own because we are the ones who caused it. You may know that in the Old Testament of the Bible God required people to sacrifice animals to redeem their sins and bridge that chasm. That may sound harsh, but sin is so serious to God that its penalty is death. The payment for sin requires either our own personal death or the death of a substitute.

The great news is that a couple thousand years ago God made a cataclysmic change by redeeming our sins and removing the separation from Him. He Himself, in the form of His Son, Jesus, came to earth as a baby through a virgin named Mary. This is the real reason we celebrate Christmas. The story doesn't end there, however.

After Jesus was born, he walked the earth and was the only person to live a sinless life and follow God's purpose in every way. At 33 years old, Jesus was put to death by people alive in that day. For more details of the amazing life and events of Jesus' life, you can read the books of Matthew, Mark, Luke and John in the Bible.

Because of Jesus' life and death on the cross, He became the ultimate sacrifice and redemption for your sin. The most exciting part is three days later Jesus rose from the dead and was seen by hundreds of witnesses who not only saw Him, but also talked with Him and even touched his wounds. Jesus did not just die like other religious leaders who are still dead. He rose again and is alive today calling you to Him.

Jesus gave us a way to be forgiven through His sinless blood shed on a cross: He died in our place. You may be familiar with John 3:16, which says, "For God so loved the world that He gave His only son so that whoever believes in Him will not perish but will have eternal life." Another verse in Romans 10 says "If you declare with your mouth, 'Jesus is Lord', and believe in your heart that God raised him from the dead, you will be saved. For it is with your heart that you believe and are justified, and it is with your mouth that you profess your faith and are saved."

This means that the most incredible thing God could ever do for you, He already did. This means that you don't have to try to face life on your own anymore but that you will be given a purpose and peace that you can never get anywhere else. It means that you want Him to lead and guide your life. It also means you want to be (and will be) with Him for eternity once you leave this earth. In order to bridge that chasm and have a relationship with your heavenly Father, all you have to do is believe. Believe that He died on the cross for you and ask Him to forgive your sins, which again are all the past things you have done

wrong in your life. When you ask Him to come into your heart, He
will, and He will change your life forever.

If you are ready to turn things over to God and live a full and adven-
turous life filled with peace and tremendous purpose for now and eternity, here is a prayer for you to pray out loud or in your heart.

"Jesus, I believe you are the Son of God and that you died for my sins,
then rose again. Thank you for loving me so much that you sacrificed
your very life. I know that I have done things in my life that were
against your will and purpose. Please forgive me. I want to start new
with you! I ask you to come into my life and lead me. I want you to
show me your way and the true purpose for which you put me on this
earth. Thank you Lord Jesus, I dedicate my life to you. Amen."

Congratulations!

You probably didn't have fireworks go off or hear a voice come down
from heaven. You may not have felt anything inside, either, but rest
assured that God heard you and He is faithful. What you will probably
notice right away, but certainly over time, is a peace inside your heart.
You are now part of the family of God, which is a huge family of other
believers you will be with for eternity.

It is important to share with someone the decision you made today.
You can share it with family or friends. If you have another Christian
in your life, I'm sure he or she would love to hear about your decision
and so would I. Please email me at hello@madetochangetheworld.com.

A next great step for you would be to attend a local church and/or
Bible study group. Make sure the place you attend is using only the
Holy Bible as their source of truth and training. Another book to help
you more clearly understand salvation and next steps is free for you at
my website or on Amazon. It is titled *Am I Saved?* Get your copy by
clicking on the Resource tab at www.madetochangetheworld.com.

Now you may have read all of this and not felt ready to make this
change or commitment. I want you to know that God loves you more
than you can comprehend! He is faithful and will keep tugging at your
heart! If you have questions or need help sorting this out, please email

me at hello@madetochangetheworld.com. You may also find great answers and insight by reading the book listed above or *The Case for Christ* by Lee Strobel.

God bless you, and remember that Jesus loves you so much that He died for you.

ACKNOWLEDGMENTS

If you have read any of my testimonial above, you will quickly see I would not even be alive today if Jesus Christ had not saved and changed me. Without Christ's perfect will and plan, I would not be here to write a book about how He has impacted my life. Thank you, Lord, for saving me through your mercy and grace on the beach that day and for daily leading me along your path through your Holy Spirit.

I would also be completely remiss if I did not thank my wife Claudia and my little Ellie. They are the most amazing two women I could ask for to live my life with. Thank you both for allowing me to spend time writing and helping others during my many busy mornings of book writing.

I am also in complete debt to some others who have been rocks in my life. They have helped me through the tough times, encouraged me with their words, and lifted me up with prayers through this book writing process. Kathy Swigle is my MTCTW partner and is a gift from heaven. Thank you, Kathy, for sticking with me and for all that you do to change the world every day. My brother-in-law Jonathan Armel is also by my side as an accountability partner and Coach. He is like my brother and a blessing from God.

There are so many others I would like to thank and acknowledge by name but that would turn this into an encyclopedia instead of one book. So I say from the bottom of my heart to my family and many friends who have supported me, encouraged me, and given me feedback over the years for my weekly message – Thank You! I cannot tell you how much your lives and encouragement mean to me.

TESTIMONIALS

The Bible is not a book to read. It is a book to live. In "Made to Change the World", Brian does just that...he inspires us to see God's instructions through the lens of small steps leading to amazing outcomes. As faith in God and coaching principles coincide, we as individuals and the church body truly have the power to change our world!

Hannah E., NBCHWC

Made to Change the World changed my life. The book helped me move closer to God, understand my purpose, and ignite a desire to help others. The information and tools enriched my relationships with family, friends, and clients.

Leslie Q., Christian Coach

I'm a Board Certified Coach and I took Brian's *Change the World* Coaching Program, and I'm so glad I did. It changed me and will help me with others' transformation process! I learned so much about what it "really" takes to be a guide on the side to someone else's change process. There aren't many coaching courses out there that incorporate the power of Christ along with this process. And the book--what a great supplement to the course and a way to further reflect on the process and go back and refresh what I learned. Yes, I plan to read that book again and again! I am thankful for knowing and experiencing the author first-hand and his Made to Change the World, partner, Kathy. Together, what a powerful team to help me help coaches who then help others. It's how we change the world! Thank you, Brian and Kathy. Forever grateful.

Cheri MC., Ph.D. Transitions Coach

A desire to change the world is a noble goal. It is a particularly important goal for the believer in Christ whose desire is to effect the kind of change that brings God the glory He is due. Most of us long to make a difference in the world, and that is where Brian Williams comes in. Made to Change the World provides the blueprint for such change in steps that are easy to understand and implement in daily life. I recommend this book for anyone who is looking to have a profound impact on the world in ways that draw others closer to God and equip them to serve Him better.

Steve E., Educator – Tampa, Florida

CHAPTER 1
THE WORLD

C hapter Focus: *I pray this book excites you about the possibilities for the rest of your life. Regardless of where you started or what you have been through, there is a big plan for you both now and forever. This first chapter is about changing your perspective. As you begin to read, be willing to stretch your mind and think bigger. Start to imagine the possibilities God has for you. Most importantly, as you read through this book, be willing to change. The ultimate purpose of "Made to Change the World" is change. Change your thinking, Grow your faith, Take new actions. As my mentor Zig Ziglar once said, "If you always do what you've always done, you'll always get what you've always got." It is time to think and do differently. Believe in God and who He made you to be. See what He does as you follow Him fully.*

THE WHEELCHAIR

As I was being released from the hospital after spending nearly two days there, I felt more than confident that I could leave on my own two legs. I was already embarrassed by being taken to the hospital by ambulance for something that ended up being just a scare. Now I was not interested in being carted out to my car in a wheelchair. I didn't get

my way. It is standard procedure that once you have been admitted to
the hospital, you have to leave by wheelchair, so they assigned
someone to come and pick me up. Jerome (as I will call him) was a
very upbeat, strong, tall man. He was probably in his early to mid-'60s
and would be my "wheelchair chauffeur."

To make matters worse, my wife couldn't carry everything to our car.
On my lap was a huge blanket a neighbor brought in for me, my wife's
large flower bag, and the hospital parting gift, which was a see-
through bag that contained a water mug, toiletries, and some other
things. Here we were going down the hall as I tried not to make eye
contact with anyone just in case someone knew me. Jerome wheeled
me to the parking circle, and there we waited for Claudia to get the car
and pick me up. I stayed there holding my huge security blanket,
flower bag, and hospital swag, and then it happened.

Jerome and I got into a long conversation. I could not help it. He was
magnetic. He knew nearly everyone who worked at the hospital and
greeted them with a warm smile and friendly hello while still paying
attention to my every need. He automatically made me feel better
about myself and this awkward situation.

As we sat there waiting, he said something that triggered me to ask if
he was a Christian, and he was. He proceeded to tell me that he could
have retired already, but he has a bigger purpose in life, which is to
bring love and joy to others through his work. He was determined to
help suffering people to feel better.

Jerome knew the meaning of suffering because seven years earlier he
was diagnosed with Hodgkin's Lymphoma, an aggressive and nasty
cancer that quickly destroys people. He was given a short time to live,
but Jerome is a fighter and trusted in God. Because of this cancer,
Jerome required a transplant to stay alive.

The day I met Jerome, I venture to guess he stood at 6'2" tall and
weighed a little over 200 pounds. At the time of his transplant operation, he weighed just over 90 pounds. He also had to stay in a medical
clinic for 16 straight months to recover. That was a year and a half of
his life in a medical facility, on chemo and fighting for his life. He said

there were days he just wanted to give up. None of us would have blamed him for it.

At one point Jerome was discouraged. Then someone cared enough to come along and motivate him. His new friend showed him how to work out to regain weight to get healthy. Jerome took his advice and regained his health, but never heard from this stranger again. Jerome believes it was an angel sent to keep him fighting for his life.

Jerome not only fought, but he also won. He is a picture of health now, beaming light to all other lives around him. Jerome is passionate about loving people and treating everyone as equals. He pays great attention to others' needs and does everything he can to make them feel better about themselves and their situations.

Jerome was given a second lease on life and is not wasting it. Every day is precious, and he has a purpose. Jerome could have retired years ago, especially after all he had been through. He realizes he is on this earth for more than just himself. Jerome is here to follow the purpose God has for him. He does this by lifting others, physically and emotionally, no matter who they are or what their background is.

As I got into the car, he helped buckle me in and said he would love to meet me again at a local store or beach, but he hoped it wouldn't be at the hospital. Jerome is real and fully living each day. He is changing the world of all those around him.

How does your current life measure up to this? I know mine doesn't, and I am the one writing a book called *Made to Change the World*. It's time for each of us to know God's purpose for our lives and to live it. There is no better way.

PERSPECTIVE

I don't know what Jerome's life was like before his near-death experience, but I know that wake-up call strengthened him inside and caused him to take a good hard look at God, his life, and his purpose here on this planet. I pray that for you reading this book it doesn't take a traumatic experience like this for you to take inventory, to draw close to God, and to live a bigger purpose.

There are many different reasons why you may have picked up Made to *Change the World*. What is your reason for wanting to read this book? It may have been a referral from someone else, or you wanted to see who was obnoxious enough to write a book with this title. You may also have a desire to change the world and make it a better place.

My hope and prayer is that by the time you finish reading *Made to Change the World* you are ready, able, and willing to be a world-changer in a new way for God. One point to clarify: When I talk about God, I am referencing Him as the Father, Son, and Holy Spirit, the triune God, with Jesus being the redemptive savior through His perfect life, death, and resurrection. For more on this, you can go to www. madetochangetheworld.com/resources and get a free copy of *Am I Saved?*.

A POWERFUL SCENE

In 2013, Mark Burnett (creator of "Survivor" and many other TV Shows) and Roma Downey released a television mini-series called "The Bible". It was a well-done dramatic interpretation of the Bible from Genesis to Revelation. All the important stories were included and it emotionally impacted each viewer as the scenes were brought to life.

One scene specifically stood out to me and still stands out to this day. It was a scene where Peter first met Jesus. Peter was a fisherman and had been trying all night to catch fish – with no success. Jesus told Peter to cast his nets on the other side of the boat and Peter doubted. How would that make any difference? He had been fishing all night, and what possible impact could putting the net on the other side of the boat have?

After some convincing, Peter did what Jesus had advised and into the net went hundreds of fish. There were so many fish that Peter had a hard time pulling them into the boat. Once he got them in, he turned to Jesus and asked how that happened. He marveled at what Jesus had just done.

Jesus lovingly turned to Peter, looked him in the eyes, and said, "I am giving you the chance to change your life. Come with me." He asked Peter to give up fishing. He said he would make him a fisher of men. Peter looked intently back at Jesus and asked: "What are we going to do?" Jesus paused, then with a look of adventure and challenge told Peter, "We are going to *change the world*." If you have not watched this 2-minute scene before, take a minute and go to www. madetochangetheworld.com to be motivated and challenged by this interaction.

We don't know if Jesus said those words, but they did come true. From that day forward, Peter and 11 other men followed Jesus into an adventure they could never have imagined with an impact that changed the world.

Think about this for a moment. What would it have been like to live back in the days when Jesus walked on the earth? Think of how it would have felt to be a person in the crowd of 5,000 who ate from the five loaves and two fish? How would you have reacted if you were the man who had his sight restored after Jesus put mud on his eyes or if you were the woman who was bleeding for many years, then touched Jesus' robe and were suddenly healed? Imagine if you had been nearby to watch Jesus raise his friend, Lazarus, from the dead. Think of the feeling under your feet if you had walked on water toward Jesus as Peter did. Jesus challenged every belief, every norm, and the very limits that our minds put on God.

Now imagine that after everything you have seen Jesus do and hear him say, the country turns against him. You are his friend. Now your friend is considered the scourge of the earth. He is prosecuted, whipped, beaten, then hung out on a cross in front of you and all the public to die. The very man you thought was God's Son that could change your country is now dead.

Now what? You find yourself in a room with other friends of His who are all shocked, in grief, and have no idea what to do. You may also be in danger because you followed Jesus, who was condemned to death. Just for being associated with him, you may be next.

Everything you hoped for is gone. What can you do now? A week earlier, you were with Jesus as He rode through the streets on a donkey with people bowing down to him. Now you are the laughing stock of the nation. There are no more miracles, no more words of wisdom, no more Jesus. It's over! The only thing you can think to do is pray and hope that from the things Jesus taught, God will show you something. Anything!

Have you ever felt like this? You put your hope in someone or something and it went opposite of what you expected. You may have even put your hope in God and it still came out very bad in your eyes. These disciples are in that place, and worse. They not only had things go wrong, they fear they will be the next ones hunted down and hung on a cross in humiliation for everyone to see. They were desperate.

Three days later something completely changed. Those three days probably felt like three years to the disciples. These men and women, who remained faithful in prayer, got to witness the miracle of all miracles. They had seen Jesus do some amazing things, but this one was something the world had never seen and never has since.

Picture yourself on the dreadful walk to a cave to go and wrap Jesus' body for burial. This would be it, the last you see of him. Soon his body would be buried in the ground along with all the hopes and dreams he had promised. Now comes the end of your hope. You get to the cave and something is wrong. The stone barrier is rolled away. How furious you would be! Not only did they kill your loving and innocent friend who changed lives, now someone has broken into the cave and stolen his body. Could things possibly get worse?

You walk up and see there is someone sitting on the rock. You are ready to rip into him and do whatever it takes to get the body back because this was the person who changed your life and turned a nation upside down through love.

This person tells you Jesus is no longer there and that he is alive. What? A week ago, this man looked to be the savior of the nation and everyone was thrilled. Three days ago, this savior was beaten and nailed to the cross, and you have been in shock and grief. Now you hear he is alive. This is the worst emotional roller coaster you can ever imagine. What can you believe? This situation is impossible!

You run into the cave and find the body is not there, but the burial clothes are. The reality of it hits you! If this is true, if Jesus actually died and is now alive, He was telling the truth. He is different from any other human being who ever walked the face of the earth. Jesus is who He said He is - the Son of God the Father. He is the Christ.

Now imagine that you are in the room when Jesus walks in on that third day, with nail marks, scars, and all left on His body. You have to believe it. He is standing there before you. This marks a new beginning for everything. Jesus completed his purpose on earth, but yours is just beginning. As Jesus later sends the Holy Spirit and ascends to the throne, His purpose as a human being on earth is complete – but yours is just getting started.

This was the life and experience of Peter and the other followers of Jesus after that day on the boat with the remarkable catch of fish. During Jesus' ministry, Jesus and the 12 disciples changed many people's lives. After Jesus' death and resurrection, Jesus changed the lives of billions of people on this planet through the lives of those who have followed Him. Jesus is still doing it to this day. Is He doing it through you?

THAT WAS THEN AND THIS IS NOW

Yes, I am getting older. The truth is, as I write this book, I am 50 years old. This is getting up there, but I am not 2,000 years old. None of us is that old, so none of us was living during the time of Jesus' birth, death, and resurrection. We can try to imagine what it was like, but we weren't there. We are here now, in this day and age more than 2,000 years later.

Many of us have gotten off track, especially in the Western culture where now our main goal is to work as hard as possible, for as short a time as possible, to retire as quickly as possible, and then lie on the beach and be served for the rest of our lives. Even when this goal is achieved, it is not fulfilling, nor it is the purpose for which we are here on this earth.

Don't get me wrong--we should enjoy life and take time to have fun, laugh, and play each day. However, this alone will never fulfill us nor achieve our purpose on this earth. Life is an adventure until the final day, and true fulfillment is not found in acquiring all you can, then withering away during retirement. You were made for more than this, so don't live what Chuck Swindoll calls a "settled-for life"

It reminds me of a friend of mine from many years ago named Ben. Ben had many reasons not to live life and feel that his life had no impact. He was born with a terminal illness. From his first breath, his days on Earth here were numbered and he would not have as many of those breaths as many of us will have through our lives.

Ben was in his early 20's when I met him and was confined to an electric wheelchair. He couldn't move his legs at all. Ben could move his arms enough to control the electronic joystick on his wheelchair to move around. He couldn't move his head much, but he could talk and smile, and that he did. He was a huge Florida Gators fan, so his dog who accompanied him always had on a Gator bandana, and Ben went to many of the games. Ben was always encouraging.

What was most impressive about Ben was that he was going to school to design racing wheelchairs. He loved the idea of faster and more mobile chairs and decided to do something to help himself and all those who use a wheelchair. He believed he was made to change the world and not just accept the hand he was dealt with tears and a "feel sorry for me" attitude.

Ben died a couple of years after we met. I am not sure how far he came along with designing his wheelchair, but it doesn't matter. His life encouraged me and many others around him to live bigger, believe more, and do all we can each day. His smile, attitude, and motivation changed me, and I realized that if I can walk, move, and live longer, I have an even bigger responsibility to live my purpose and to impact this world. As Luke 12:48 says, "To whom much is given much is required."

Before moving any further into this book, let's take three minutes to find how much of a world changer you are (or think you could be). Simply go to www.madetochangetheworld.com/assessment to take the assessment. I promise it will take you three minutes at most and is an important first step in building your awareness. Remember to take it again to see where you find yourself six or twelve months down the road.

NOW WHAT?

Now that you have taken the assessment, you have most likely become aware of something new. You may already be very clear about your life purpose and passion and are actively living it. However, if you are like most, life direction and purpose is very unclear. It makes daily life feel like driving on an unlit and foggy road at night with no headlights and trying to find the way.

The original title of this book was *How to Change the World*, and I was cruising on the manuscript until God put a stop to it. I was frustrated for months because I had set my timeline for the book and it did not happen. Why this hold up? After searching and praying and feeling stuck, God showed me the reason. I was coming at this book the wrong way and I had to switch the focus.

The original purpose for the book was to help you figure out what in the world you want to change, but it has been re-written to help you know the truth, believe the truth, then live it fearlessly for God as He calls you to. The situation with many of us is that we don't believe we can have an impact on this world, nor do we know how to live out our life's purpose in confidence. God did not put you on this earth for 70 or 80 years to be miserable, barely get through life, then die. God put you on this earth for an exciting purpose--one that is fulfilling to you and will positively impact the world around you.

As you read this book, I encourage you to take notes, highlight, re-read, and absorb the content. Most importantly – pray and take action! Use all the tools I recommend and provide through www.

madetochangetheworld.com. Life is an adventure – it's time to start living life and not just barely getting through it hoping that you make it to the end.

AUDACIOUS IDEA

As I write this book, my full-time career is running a large coaching division at a wellness company. Over the years, I have personally helped thousands of people get healthy, lose weight, and eat better. The coaches I have trained and led have now helped hundreds of thousands of people, which is exciting and impactful. As I stated in the introduction, about one week before my birthday I had this thought, which was, *"I am helping a lot of people live longer, but how many people am I helping live forever?"* Ouch! It felt like a jab to the face, or at least my heart.

The reason I got into coaching in the first place was because of powerful life situations from my past that caused me to make changes in my own life. As I shared in my testimony earlier about wanting to end my life and pleading with God, He kept His promises. My life was not, however, a Hallmark card. While you might think the story ended here and life was happy-ever-after, just the opposite occurred!

A couple of months later I had taken a personality test at the church I was attending. It said I couldn't do anything in life. It also told me that I had no confidence, no energy, no leadership skills, no management ability, and could not speak in front of others. I also was informed that I could not take on any job that really called for much interaction with others and that I didn't even have the confidence to discipline kids. Thanks a lot, personality test. As if I wasn't already feeling depressed, this sure put the icing on the cake. I was about ready to revisit taking my life.

I received these test results in a counselor's office at church. He left the room to let me consider the findings. As I sat there reading the summary, I called out to God, whom I had just committed to following a few months earlier. I said, "What the heck is this all about?" I will never forget the response that I heard. In my head God's voice clearly said, "This is who you are, but it is not who I made you to be!"

Although God's answer was somewhat comforting, I didn't know what that meant. I still planned to keep my commitment I made at the beach of daily praying and reading the Bible, but there was no specific direction telling me what to do or what to change.

Over the ten years following that fateful day, I took "leaps of faith" to follow what I felt God was calling me to do. I acted in plays, spoke in front of groups, worked in sales, led teams, and more. I did not realize what was happening until I reread the original personality test and found that God led me to do everything the personality test said I could not and should not do. Now my life was fulfilling and worth living. It was the opposite of what I had originally believed about myself and my future. I now had a bigger purpose and a deeper faith.

Most people, especially Christians, live lives full of fear, regrets, and lies they have come to believe over the years. My passion then became helping others overcome these huge pitfalls. I wanted to give back and help others know, believe, and live their true purpose. I desired to help them live an adventure and make an impact in this world, so I became a full-time life coach. Ironically, that type of career is another thing the original test said I could never do.

Although my career today is focused on health and wellness, my purpose goes more in-depth than helping people live longer; it is to help people live fuller lives and live forever. It is also to help you impact the world as you live your purpose.

What is your impact on this world?

If you cannot answer that question positively and with the confidence that God is happy with how you live each day, it is time to reevaluate. Your life matters. You are not on this earth to simply exist and live a somewhat fulfilling life. You are not a mistake. The exact day and time that you are here on this earth is not an accident. You are important, and you mean more than you can possibly know to the God who created the universe. It's time to stop believing lies that you learned through your life. It's time to stop just getting by with little confidence in what you do and trust the Holy Spirit's power within you. It is time for you to take responsibility to become who God made you to be. It's time to step up to change yourself and the world around you.

Why is your life so important? Because the world is getting worse instead of better. This seems contrary to what should be happening because as of this writing, 75% of the United States population considers themselves to be Christian. This means that nearly a quarter of a billion people in the U.S. alone, the most affluent and influential country in the world, believe in God and believe Jesus Christ to be His Son and Savior of all.

Yet morals are disappearing, abuse is rising, and killing runs rampant. Most people now speak with hate instead of love. Things are happening just in the United States alone that we know break God's heart.

Now imagine that each of us who make up that 75% completely lived full out for God in every area of our lives. What kind of impact and influence would this have in the United States? In the world? Unlike many other countries on earth, there is not a huge need in the U.S. to teach who Jesus is. The real need is for each of us to truly live what we say we believe.

There is a song written by a Christian artist named Matthew West titled "Do Something". It hits home about God's purpose for you here on this earth. Here are the lyrics:

I woke up this morning

Saw a world full of trouble now, thought

How'd we ever get so far down, and

How's it ever gonna turn around

So I turned my eyes to Heaven

I thought, "God, why don't You do something?"

. . .

WELL, I JUST COULDN'T BEAR THE THOUGHT OF

People living in poverty

Children sold into slavery

The thought disgusted me

So, I shook my fist at Heaven

Said, "God, why don't You do something?"

He said, "I did, yeah, I created you" (now listen)

If not us, then who

If not me and you

Right now, it's time for us to do something, yeah

If not now, then when

Will we see an end

To all this pain

Oh, it's not enough to do nothing

It's time for us to do something

THE PULL

As you read this first chapter, things may have stirred in you. I hope they did. You may have watched the video on the front page of www.madetochangetheworld.com and gotten chills by Jesus' words. I hope you did. You may have been able to relate to some of my testimony and know those feelings. You may have read the song above and become motivated to do something. These are all great, but now what?

It is not too hard for me to write a book about being created to change the world. It is also not extremely difficult to produce a video or write a song about faith if that is something God has gifted you to do. It is not even difficult to share your life's story with someone else. What is quite difficult is to live every day sold out in faith to know, believe, and follow God – that's tough! I will never forget the quote of a client who became a Christian through our coaching who said, "The biggest challenge with being a Christian is daily surrender." Even for the portion of the 75% of Christians who try to live daily for God, it is not easy, as this world continually pulls the other direction on us.

I got a visual of this in my mind at a recent birthday party. We had put up some helium balloons that were tied by strings to party chairs and tables. There was an undeniable pull from inside the balloon to go higher and higher. It wanted to release the grasp of my hand and leave. It was the helium within the balloon that normally exists at a much higher elevation in the atmosphere. The thing holding the helium down was the rubber encasing of the balloon and the string. If the helium had its way, it would escape from the balloon and rise. The helium doesn't even want to take the balloon with it. It just wants to go home.

That is how we feel at times with our spirit entrapped in these bodies. The spirit within us, brought alive by the Holy Spirit, wants to go home. However, it is held in this casing called our physical body that traps it here on this earth for a short time. God designed a brain, heart, lungs, hands, feet, and many other contraptions to allow our spirit to live and move on this planet earth. However, once the truth becomes alive in us, we feel the tension or pull of this world and the longing to be home in Heaven.

God didn't haphazardly give you life and a body with a spirit living in it. You were known and planned from the beginning of time. There is a purpose for you. A plan to be unveiled for you to live a life of joy and adventure here on this earth (in your balloon casing) until the day you go to be with the Lord in heaven.

As a side note, the helium that is stuck in the balloon also has a purpose until it is released into the atmosphere. The balloon is a signal to the world that there is a party getting started. It announces where the celebration is and who is being celebrated. It brings great joy to children who get to hold and play with it as it rises above for all to see.

Who can argue against the fun of taking in a breath of helium and then talking?

One day you will go to be with the Lord Jesus Christ in Heaven. You will stand in front of God the Father along with billions of others and God will ask you questions. One of those questions may be about how well you lived your purpose here on this earth. If God didn't have a plan for you on this planet today – you would not be here.

The way you live your life as a Christian each day comes down to three things: 1) What you really know about God and the power He has given you on this earth, 2) Your willingness to accept the truth of God for your own life, 3) Your commitment to live full out for God based on faith alone. These will be our next three chapters.

Bible Verse:

MATTHEW 4:19-20 – "'COME, FOLLOW ME,' JESUS SAID, 'AND I WILL SEND you out to fish for people.' At once they left their nets and followed him.'"

Prayer:

Lord Jesus, You made the world, then you came to live with us in order to change it! You came to save me and challenge me to change the world, also. Help me to think bigger, believe more, and be the person you called me to be. As I live for you, let my life be a light to draw others to you. In Jesus's name, Amen.

Take Action:

1. If you have not already done so, go to www.madetochangetheworld.com and take the short assessment to learn your starting point.
2. Get a notepad or journal and start capturing your answers to

the questions asked in this book as you continue to read. It can be life-changing.

3. Consider using additional tools and resources offered at www. madetochangetheworld.com/resources to help you grow and change as you read.

Additional Resources:

Book - *The Purpose Driven Life* – By Rick Warren

Movie – *The Bible* – By Mark Burnett and Roma Downey

Music – "Do Something" – By Matthew West

Tool – *World Changer Assessment* at www.madetochangetheworld.com/assessment

CHAPTER 2
YOUR LIFE MATTERS

C **hapter Focus:** *This chapter is focused on your purpose and the plan God has for you. It can be easy to feel lost or insignificant in this world, but there is an important reason God put you on earth right now. Many people live what Charles Stanley calls a "settled-for life". If you ever feel that way, don't worry. The true-life that is worth living is led by purpose, not by accident. Keep your mind open to what God wants to show you about the reason He put you on this earth. As you read this chapter, you will find your purpose becoming clear as you begin to focus on the one thing at the very core of who you are.*

IT'S ABOUT YOU

"Made to Change the World" is not about everyone else. It's about you. If there is one thing I hope you get from reading this book, it is that you would know and believe just how important your life is. You may have read Chapter 1 and thought about how great those stories are for Jerome, Ben, and even Peter, but that you are nothing special. The fact is, you are something special--really special. God says so!

There is a great purpose for you on this earth. There is a reason why you are alive right now, at this place in history, and reading this book. It is time for you to break free of the limits you place on yourself and live completely upon the unlimited strength and promises of God. Every person you have read about and will read about in this book is just like you. No one on this earth is more valuable than anyone else in God's eyes, and your value does not lie in what you do, but in who you are.

LESSONS FROM THE LION KING

In 1994 Walt Disney Pictures released one of the most popular movies of all time called *The Lion King*. The story starts by showing Mufasa, the king of the lion pride at the time, ruling over an area of Africa. The movie quickly turns into the account of his young cub son named Simba having to grow up quickly and try to figure out life and learn who he is. If you have not seen the original movie, I recommend watching it. If you have not seen the remake, which is called a photorealistic animated film (released in July of 2019), I highly recommend checking it out. It teaches many great life lessons.

As the movie opens, a powerful song called "Circle of Life" grabs emotions. The visual of Mufasa and his wife, Sarabi standing near the edge of a cliff called Pride Rock does, too. They are overlooking a vast land in Africa. All the other animals in the region have come to witness what is going to take place. Just then, Rafiki, a funny-looking primate called a Mandrill, gets ready to introduce to the world an important new lion cub. This new life is the son of the king, and his name is Simba. Rafiki takes the little cub and lifts him above his head at the top of Pride Rock for all the animals to see. As Rafiki dedicates and blesses little Simba, all the crowd cheers and bows down to their future king.

I bet you can picture the scene in your mind. You can probably remember a part of the song and have possibly even felt some emotion. The amazing thing is, it's all fake. It is a great story created through Hollywood magic. Disney connects you to a symbolic idea of how animals would act if they could talk and think like humans.

There is, however, a true-life story more powerful than this scene in *The Lion King*. It's about your life. There was a day that you decided to accept Jesus into your heart as your King, and the most amazing thing happened. You did not just become His "subject"; you became His child. As the Bible describes, you were "born again". This is amazing and fantastic. Do you understand what this means? Is it as impactful in your mind as the opening scene in *The Lion King*?

Let's turn this into a movie scene of your life. In Luke 15:10 (NIV), Jesus says, "In the same way, I tell you, there is rejoicing in the presence of the angels of God over one sinner who repents." Imagine that God the Father and Jesus are on top of a grand ledge looking out among all the angels in heaven. There is a worship song being sung by all the angels, and you are there with this heavenly host. At the time you accept Jesus into your heart, the Holy Spirit lifts you for all of heaven to see, and every being goes wild with cheers and thanks and tears acknowledging you as the child of the king. It is no small event. Although the things of this earth may not have made a big deal out of your decision, all of heaven did, and still does! You are the child of the King.

In *The Lion King* movie, not long after this fantastic celebration, Simba finds himself lost in this big world. As he starts to grow up, He tries to find out who He is and is having a hard time. What does being the son of the king mean? He feels like a failure and never wants to claim his rightful place in the pride. Then, at one point, his deceased father appears to him through a vision and says, "remember who you are." He proclaims that Simba is his son and the rightful air and that he is to go and take his place in the world.

Unfortunately, most Christians, soon after accepting Jesus in their hearts, get lost in life immediately following the celebration. You may have done this or still do this. You try to figure out who you are and what it means to be the son of the King for life on this earth. To borrow the line from *The Lion King*, "Remember who you are", and whose you are, and take your place. Do not let fear, worry, doubt, or anything else hold you back from being who you are. Don't let feelings or lies hold you back from the amazing life God has in store for you. Take your place in this world. Regardless of your past, your failures, or even successes. God has more planned for you, his child, than you know.

I won't spoil the movie if you haven't seen it, but I will say Simba faces his past. He decides to stand up to the circumstances, to stand up for who he is and who he is called to be. He faces his fears and takes on his greatest challenge by taking his intended place in life. In doing so, there is an internal battle within him and an external battle with the evil that Simba must face to realize who he is. His life then has its greatest meaning.

This book covers key points for life, such as learning and living by the truth. You will learn about what to put in place to walk close with God and hear His voice. You will learn how to live for God in ways that He will bless all that you do. However, none of this matters if you don't know and believe in who you are.

It does not matter where you have been or what you have done. It does not matter what anyone else thinks of you. It doesn't even matter what you believe about yourself. What matters most is to realize that God, the maker of the universe, made you and put you on this earth right now for a huge purpose. He loves you not for what you do, but for who you are. He will lead you past all fears, all failures, all insecurities into a life of adventure with Him. One that will be fulfilling to you because you please God. It will also be a life that impacts everyone around you in a way that changes this world. Remember who you are, and whose you are, the child of the King. It is time to take your place.

FINDING YOUR PURPOSE

A vague description of how to take your place in this world and impact the people around you means nothing. You need to know precisely how to apply this to your life. It reminds me of a quote from Steven Covey in his book *Seven Habits of Highly Effective People*, which says that "many people climb the ladder of success only to get to the top and find that their ladder is against the wrong wall." Not only do you want your ladder in life to be against the right wall, but you also want it to be the right ladder.

To describe the importance of life purpose, several years ago Pastor Rick Warren illustrated it by holding up a strange-looking tool in front of the congregation and asking if anyone knew what it was or what it does. Out of thousands in attendance, not one person raised a hand. He went on to explain that the tool was for a unique purpose in construction. If you try using the tool for the wrong purpose, like hammering a nail, it was very ineffective. However, when used as designed, the device was fantastic for completing the specific job for which it was created. This is the same with your life. If you want to have a fulfilled life and achieve a great purpose here on this earth, you have to ask the Maker why you are here and how to use your skills, abilities, and passion to fulfill your unique purpose.

The definition of purpose is "The reason for which something is done or created or for which something exists." Purpose is more than a phrase or an idea. It is the center of all the things in your life. Your purpose determines what you do and why you do it.

In this day and age, there are countless books, videos, and teachings about how to have success in life and fulfill your purpose. If there is a purpose in this life and this world, what is it and why does it seem so hard to find? The answer is that there is a great purpose God has for you in this world. The foundational purpose for everything you do, think, and strive for as a Christian can be narrowed down to one word.

Before I mention that one word, let me share a story. This true story is about my three-year-old daughter, Ellie. You will hear more about her through this book in other illustrative stories, but let me tell you about those early days. The first time I held her, I could not believe that God would trust me with this tiny human life. I remember thinking to myself that I must support her back and head, and, most importantly, to not drop her. *Whatever you do, don't drop her!* My wife even has a picture of that moment with a clear look on my face of "don't drop the baby". Thankfully, I didn't.

I realized that already contained within this tiny baby is everything she will need for her life. She has a body, a heartbeat, a brain. She has lungs, which was quite obvious every time she cried and is still quite obvious to this day. She was tiny, tender, and fragile. She was a brand-new human that would one day grow up to be and do things that only God knows.

She was helpless. She was beautiful. She could do absolutely nothing on her own. The early days were critical for us to get to know her and find what she needs. We had to take care of her. To learn about her needs and tendencies and pay attention to every little thing. It took self-sacrifice and many sleepless nights. At that time, she could give us nothing in return. She was trying to stay alive and figure out this new world.

We did all of these things for our little girl and still do today based on one thing, which is love. Claudia and I love Ellie with all of our hearts, and no matter what she does, we choose to love her and always will. We may not be happy with all the things she does, but our love and caring for her is not based on what she does. It is based on who she is.

Love is our purpose on earth. From the day we were created, and every day after, love is at our core. We were made to love and to be loved. That is God's purpose for you. That is why He made the world: because of love.

When Jesus was asked what is the greatest commandment in all of the world, His answer was this: Luke 10:27 (NIV) "'Love the Lord your God with all your heart, and with all your soul, and with all your strength and with all your mind'; and, 'Love your neighbor as yourself.'"

Here are key points to realize about these words as translated from the original Greek:

The word "heart" means passion and emotions.

The word "soul" means your desires and will.

The word "mind" means your thinking and logic.

The word "strength" means your actions and body.

To put it another way, Jesus is saying to love God with all your thoughts, emotions, and desires, which will guide your actions. Let everything that goes through your mind be based on God's truth. Let your emotions be subjected to passionately loving God. Let the greatest determination of your life be following God's purpose and plan. Finally, let the things you do with your body glorify God by basing them on right thinking, emotions, and determination.

In addition to loving God, we are also called to love our neighbors. We automatically default to "loving" ourselves but not others. God is saying that we should make the hopes, dreams, feelings, and desires of others just as important as your very own.

It is easy to say and write that the purpose of life is to love! Even the Beatles wrote a popular song about it back in the 1960s called "All You Need is Love". Technically, that is true. The problem is that everyone's interpretation of what love is can be quite different, so here is what love is, from God's perspective, and how to know if you are basing your life on love or on something, or someone, else.

First, here is what love is not:

Love is not merely an emotion; it is a choice.

Love is not romance or sex (in this context); it is brotherly love.

Love is not selective; it loves everyone.

Here are other things that love is not, based on 1 Corinthians 13:4-7:

Love "… does not envy, it does not boast, it is not proud. It does not dishonor others, it is not self-seeking, it is not easily angered, it keeps no record of wrongs. Love does not delight in evil…"

Secondly, Here is what love is, again based on 1 Corinthians 13:4-7:

"Love is patient, love is kind." Love also "… rejoices with the truth. It always protects, always trusts, always hopes, always perseveres." Love is always victorious.

Love is giving.

Love values others.

Ultimately, God is love! (1 John 4:7)

Now let's see how you are doing in these areas. Look at the list below and consider the way you mainly treat all people in your life. For each line below, circle the one you generally default to in life. Be truthful if you want to see how well you love and fulfill your purpose. Then add up how many you have in the "What love is not" column and the "What love is" column.

Love is not...

Emotion-based

Subjective

Taking

Envious

Boastful

Proud

Dishonoring

Self-seeking

Easily angered

Holding a grudge

Delighted with evil

Being defeated

Love is...

Truth based

Valuing everyone

Giving

Grateful

Hopeful

Humble

Kind

Protecting others

Patient

Forgiving

Rejoicing with truth

Victorious

IMAGINE WHAT LIFE WOULD BE LIKE IF EVERYONE LIVED LIFE BASED ON THE *What Love Is* list. What would your relationships be like? What would your town and country look like? How would this world change? It all starts with one person--you--making an effort to follow God and live a life of love. Here is an example from my life years ago.

I was feeling stuck and in a grind at a job where I was working just five years out of college. I worked for a financial firm in Southern California as a Financial Planner, and after a few years in that position, I wanted to move on. I was unhappy with the situation at the office and started focusing on my feelings of discontent. I was discouraged and wanted a change. You may be able to relate to this situation from some time in your life.

As I prayed, I kept feeling that I needed to stay in that position for some reason. It was uncomfortable, but I stayed. I kept a good attitude by focusing on God and His plan until I realized why He had me there. I will never forget the day after New Year's coming back into the office and sitting at lunch with a co-worker of mine whom I will call Susan. As she began to weep, we talked and she filled me in about her life and the many hardships she was going through. I listened, I comforted her, and I shared the good news about Jesus. She decided right there to give her life over to Him as her Lord and Savior.

Soon after her commitment to Jesus, her attitude and life started to change. She found a church, a boyfriend (who became her husband), a new job, and later ended up having a family. It was all worth it. This was why God had me stay at the office. I didn't know why and was feeling frustrated, but I was responsible for sticking to God's purpose and maintaining the right attitude while God had me there. I had to be available and listening at the right time. This all led to changing Susan's life forever. The purpose of my struggle was much bigger than my feelings. It was to be used to impact someone's life for eternity, and I thank God for using me to help her.

LOST IN A CROWD

How to find a way to feel like you are having an impact in this world through love is a challenge. You are in a crowd, but don't get lost. God knows exactly where you are and what He has planned for you. It is for a great reason that you must live your purpose. Here is an illustration.

As of 2019, it is estimated that there are 7,530,000,000 people in the world. To put that into perspective, if you have ever been to an American football game or watched one on TV, the average seating capacity of an NFL stadium is nearly 70,000 people. Right now, the United States has 140 significant stadiums, which would hold a total of 9,800,000 people. To seat the world's population, we would have to build an additional 108,290 stadiums. That would mean filling up the cities of New York, Los Angeles, Chicago, Atlanta, San Diego, Houston, Miami, San Francisco, and Seattle with only stadiums and no other buildings to hold everyone. For all you football fans, I am sure that would be a dream come true.

Imagine now that was the case with more than 100,000 stadiums, back to back, in these cities, and you get one ticket to go to one stadium and sit in one seat. That is your spot in this world. I don't know about you, but I would feel like an insignificant life in a sea of billions of other people. I wouldn't think I had a chance to be the one guy who gets called down to the field to try to throw a football to win a new car. I wouldn't even think I had the chance to be in the section that wins a free hot dog.

We can feel insignificant in light of the masses of people in the world around us. What is the impact you or I can have? If we were in one of the full stadiums and stood up to ask for help, how many people would hear us? More importantly, how many would respond? People two sections over would not know who we are or what we need. Those in other stadiums wouldn't even have a clue that we existed. This is where our Christian faith and our trust in God come in!

Somehow and some way, God knows exactly who you are, where you are, and what is happening in your life. He also knows why you are here on this earth today. He has a plan for you--a big plan--to have an impact on this world right there from the very seat where you sit. God has you in the exact right place, in the exact right stadium and at the exact right time right now. This does not mean all your circumstances are ideal and that you know where He will ultimately lead you to be, but it means He has opportunities for you to live your purpose and impact others this very day.

Picture yourself now in this football stadium and sitting in your seat. Instead of thinking how lost you may be in that crowd, think about the person sitting directly beside you, behind you, and in front of you. Those people are important, and they have real needs to be loved and taken care of. God has you in a place of impact. He may not be calling you to be the announcer or a player on the field. He is calling you to be you and to realize that your very life is to love and influence directly around you.

When Peter followed Jesus, he probably didn't think about the world's population, all the troubles that they could come up against or the final fate of Jesus. He was inspired to follow a man who was different and who had a purpose.

We have a short time to be on this earth. It is an important responsibility. God has given you life to live it in the most meaningful way possible. Your life is important! Changing the world means to change the world around you through love by being exactly who you were made to be and doing what you are designed to do every day.

THE RIPPLE EFFECT

About a year ago, when my daughter Ellie was two, we were in my parents' backyard standing near their pond. It was very calm water with no real movement until I threw a little stone into the middle. Ellie watched the ripples go all through the pond and hit every shore. When I threw a bigger rock in, the ripples were even larger and changed the water once again. Your life and the way you live it has a ripple effect every day for those around you.

Something we must each examine is this: What are all the ripple effects we are causing? We may be making a positive ripple in our career by helping others, yet having a very negative ripple effect by abusing our family at home. You could love your family, yet promote things online or in the workplace that hurt others and tear them down. No matter what you are doing now or have done previously in this world, it causes a ripple effect. In every area of your life, the key is to intentionally create a ripple effect that is Godly and loving.

I will never forget a card I received and still have, from a man with whom I had an initial coaching call some years before. In his card, he wrote that our 45-minute discussion changed his life, and he proceeded to tell me about all the things he had changed in his personal, family, and business life since then. I don't remember all the details of our discussion, but he was grateful by the end of our call. I had taken the time and listened to God regarding what to say, and the ripple effect went from this man to his family to his co-workers and probably countless others.

Think about this – it is the seemingly small things you do, words you say, and actions you take that will change a life and you don't realize it. Everything you do causes a ripple in this world. You are either creating productive waves, or they are destructive like a flood.

Is the size and impact of your current ripple effect what you want it to be? Most of us would say "no" to this question right now. I personally have impacted thousands through coaching to help people improve their lives and health, and still feel my ripple is nowhere near where I want it to be. The great news is there is more--much more--to come. Here is an example of a person who seemed to have no possibility of causing a ripple in this world. However, because she follows God, her ripple continues even long after her death.

Several years ago, there lived an Albanian woman named Anjeze Gonxhe Bojaxhiu. She was born in a small, underdeveloped country with an ordinary start to life. She originally had trouble finding her purpose and almost lost her faith in God and direction in life because of it. Talk about having a little ripple or none at all. However, she decided to persevere and move forward by dedicating herself to helping others – one person at a time. Most of us know this woman as Mother Teresa.

During her time on earth, the world was full of large-scale challenges and problems regarding poverty, disease, sickness, etc. India rose to the top of the list of challenged nations. Calcutta was not known for affluence and easy living. It was, however, known for poverty and disease. This is where Mother Teresa decided to pursue her purpose. Her focus was to bring dignity and peace to the sick so they would not die alone or be rejected. Her goal was outreach to the poorest of the poor. She had no desire to be a world heroine; she just wanted to help the little section of people around her.

She believed God had a calling on her life and she "practiced what she preached." What she did during her 87 years on earth was anything but easy. She had some dark and doubtful days, but had a common quote that she lived by: *"Give your hands to serve and your heart to love."*

Genty-Akin said Mother Teresa prayed each day asking for God's light to shine through her so that those who came in contact with her would "see no longer me but only Jesus." She prayed this prayer even during the many times she felt God had abandoned her, and she remained faithful to Him and His calling throughout her life. Mother Teresa was not focused on making good impressions but on meeting the needs of others.

Mother Teresa's impact on the world, even after her passing, is that 5,000 sisters of her order in 762 convents in 135 countries are still carrying out the work she established. Whether you are called to be a leader like Mother Teresa or a teammate like these 5,000 or a contributor to the cause as someone who gives time, money, or energy to a great purpose, you are called.

You may already have known of Mother Teresa and her impact. You may also be thinking, *"I am not Mother Teresa, nor do I believe I ever will be. If that is what I need to do to have an impact on this world then I should give up now."*

Rest assured, that is not everyone's call because we each have different skills, abilities, and gifts to use. There is only one Mother Teresa, and there is only one you! Be inspired about how to love and impact the section of people around you.

LIVING YOUR PURPOSE

Ultimately, the change in this world comes from you and me. Who knows what you can do to impact the world and its struggling people? There are multitudes of us who will never be written in history books, but we will be known by God and every person around us whose lives we have impacted by fully dedicating ourselves to loving God and loving the people around us. Think of a person in your life who greatly impacted you but will never get a Purple Heart or accolades for what he or she has done.

There is a world changer you probably have never heard of before. Claudia was born in the underdeveloped country of Mexico and was raised by God-fearing parents. She grew up in an oppressed and immoral culture driven by greed and corruption. In the mid-1990s, her parents moved her family to the United States by faith, in hopes of greater opportunity and a chance to have a bigger impact on this world. They had to adapt to a new culture, learn a new language, and overcome fear.

Claudia worked hard after coming to the United States by going into the dental field. She ended up learning and working in all areas of the business including sales, management, organization, and marketing. Claudia developed impactful methods to run an office and operate at peak efficiency. She started as a dental assistant and eventually worked her way up to managing a large dental practice with many employees.

Claudia impacted those around her through encouragement and professional skill-building to help them grow in their lives and careers. She loved her team, and every chance she had, she shared the love of God with them. You probably never heard of her, but if you live in Orange County, California, you may have been impressed by her or one of her teammates while going in for dental visits.

Running a dental office with over twenty employees, thousands of patients, and millions of dollars in revenue is a purposeful and impactful career. She was living her purpose and had a tremendous impact for good on the world she was helping. However, in 2017 her family grew with a new baby and was headed for a difficult and challenging life situation with juggling a career and being a mom. Claudia decided to quit her job and go full time with her new daughter. She now spends every day with Ellie embracing the struggles and challenges that come with raising a baby. Every day, Ellie experiences the love of a mother who lives a Godly life and loves her baby, takes her to church, and teaches her about God. Ellie is growing, and so is her mom.

You would think that Claudia had a more significant impact on the world by working in the dental field interacting with all her co-workers and thousands of patients. This is not the case. The effect of one is world-changing. This change in "career" makes all the difference in the world. Who knows what that baby will grow up to be and do? She may grow up to influence multitudes because of her mother's chosen purpose to give all she has to love her.

Claudia is one of my heroes in life. She lives for God, walks by faith and is changing the World every day! I know this because Claudia has lived selflessly each day as my wife for over 20 years. Thank you, my love, for all you do for me and your family each day.

I tell you this story because you may think the only way to change the world is to be the President of the United States or the head of the United Nations. This is not true. In actuality, those leaders have much less of an impact on this world than you have directly on another person's life by living your purpose and loving the way God wants.

Loving and influencing those directly around you is your most significant impact on this earth.

You may be called to affect the lives of thousands of people, or maybe one person. The number of people doesn't matter, but the influence does. Only by living your purpose will you find out the full impact of what God wants to do through you in this world. It doesn't start with how you live in one area of your life. It starts by living all areas of your life for God. As you do so, what comes out of who you are and how you live will emanate to the people around you.

IMPACT THE WORLD BY CHANGING YOURSELF

Like the pebble thrown into a calm lake that makes ripples in the water and spreads throughout the whole lake, so, too, is the impact of your life. However, the ripple you can make in this world doesn't start with trying to change everyone. It begins with changing yourself by living a life of love that will fulfill your purpose for being on this earth.

Because this may be hard to conceptualize, here are some specific examples of the impact you may have on the world around you when deciding to change your own life:

- Deciding to take responsibility for your part in a failed relationship by acknowledging your shortfall and forgiving the other person
- Recognizing when someone around you needs help, whether you know them or not, then providing that help
- Volunteering your time at a church or organization to help those who are in need
- Giving some/more of your hard-earned finances to those who are much less fortunate
- Getting support from a counselor or coach to move past the things that have held you back your whole life
- Being the person at work who is always supportive, positive, and goes the extra mile for others
- Starting a ministry, idea or project that helps others grow and change in life

- Taking care of your spouse, your child, and your family with love and patience in all you do
- Taking steps to set new goals that will have a positive impact on you and the world around you
- Committing yourself to God and following His plan each day of your life
- Learning to love and show love to those around you (in word and deed)
- Listening--truly listening--to others
- Asking God to lead you to impact what you listed at the beginning of this book that you want to see changed in this world

If you want to see your nation and this world changed for the good, here is a promise from God: "If my people, who are called by my name, will humble themselves and pray, and seek my face and turn from their wicked ways, then I will hear from heaven, and I will forgive their sin and will heal their land" (2 Chronicles 7:14).

What is your purpose here on this earth? Yes, it is to love, but how are you going to do that? In all of my years in helping people find and follow God's purpose for them, a great starting point is to write your purpose statement. A personal purpose statement is not about what you will do but who you are, in Christ, which leads to how you live life. I quote mine every morning to help me focus on my purpose and live it each day.

I also have written a mission statement, which is how I will live my purpose in this world, along with a vision statement about what living this way will lead to in life. If you have not taken the time to write these out for yourself, I highly recommend it as the first step in clarifying who you are and how you will love in this world.

I have created some excellent resources for you to explore and articulate your purpose, mission, and vision. I wrote a book several years back called *Directions for Life,* which can be found on Amazon or by going to www.madetochangetheworld.com/resources. There is also a companion workbook available at the website shown above. You can also benefit from signing up for weekly Made to Change the World emails that provide free tools for all the different areas covered in this book. The most powerful way to get help with not only formulating your statements but living them out in your life is to work with an MTCTW Coach, which you can find at www. madetochangetheworld.com/coaching.

IMAGINE FOR A MOMENT

We talked about both the stadium and the ripple effect in comparison to life purpose. Now picture yourself in your seat and in the stadium God has set for you. Imagine that you know your purpose and how to love in this world, you've set your mission of how you will do it, and you are excited about the impact God will have through you. Now you turn your sights to the small group of people around you in your little section. You are going to love them in the way God designed and gifted you.

If you are married, your spouse is right near you in your section. If you have kids, they are also sitting close. You may have one or more living parents who are in your area in this stadium. Your section also may include brothers and sisters, neighbors, co-workers, friends, and all others with whom you frequently interact.

As you live your purpose, it will start a small ripple into others' lives. They will begin to experience love, trust, and hope in a new way. Your little ripple could start to cause a ripple in them. Maybe not immediately and perhaps not even visible, but God will begin that work in and through you to impact them.

This small ripple will produce other small ripples of others deciding they also want to live their purpose for God. Small ripple after small ripple creates more ripples in the lives of others in your section and possibly other sections in your little stadium. You may start to realize that the small ripples could turn into waves over time.

You may have been in a stadium where the wave started. The whole concept of the wave at a game is a small group of people deciding to stand up, then sit down. Others around them see it and then follow.

After several attempts at starting this wave, it catches on and soon all the sections around the stadium are forming a wave of unison that looks amazing as you sit and watch it.

As background, the supposed history of the stadium wave is credited to a man named Krazy George Henderson. Although the exact day and origin of the very first wave activity is not agreed upon by everyone, the first video-recorded event of the wave was at a Major League Baseball game on October 15, 1981 in Oakland, California. Once everyone across the country saw the wave occur, it began sweeping through stadiums across the United States and the world. One little ripple turned into a wave that later caught on in event after event for many decades.

Wherever you find yourself right now is the very section where God wants you to start. Live for Him, love others, and start the little ripple just like the stone I threw in the water with Ellie that eventually made it through the whole pond. You may not even see the small ripple you are causing, but God says that His Word will not return void and when you speak His Word in love to others, you are beginning an eternal ripple effect.

You don't have to plan to persuade thousands of people to change to make an impact in this word. Commit to becoming the person you were designed to be, and commit to loving God, others, and yourself. As you persevere through the tough times, your impact will be world-changing.

One example of a small ripple happening in my life is the very book you are reading. As I write, I have no idea if anyone will read the end product. I am hoping at least those closest to me will. I am also hoping it stirs in them something that creates a new ripple of how God wants to use them. Possibly the ripple of this book will get bigger and create a wave that will spread to more people to cause a ripple in them.

In doing what God calls you to do, you are not in charge of the ripple effect. You are responsible for following God's plan. The result of you doing what God calls you to do will be a ripple effect. I may not even be one who sees you during your time here on earth, but God does.

Have faith that He will use your obedience to impact others. Don't focus on changing the stadium. Focus on God and the opportunities He has placed around you to fulfill His purpose and plan; the result will be up to Him.

THE IMPORTANCE OF YOUR PURPOSE

Jentezen Franklin tells a story that has been handed down through the years. The exact details of this written story may be slightly different from what really happened, but the point is powerful. The story is about a man many years ago who was driving along the road and his car broke down. He had to pull over and try to fix it.

To the man's surprise as he struggled with the car, a limousine pulled up behind him to stop and help. A man got out of the limo dressed like a million dollars. He asked if he could be of assistance. The owner of the car was more than happy to get additional help. After a few minutes of tinkering under the hood, the man from the limousine had the vehicle fully functioning again.

The grateful car owner asked how he could repay the man. The helpful man from the limo said it was no cost. Then he went on to say his name was Henry Ford and he was the creator of that car. He added, "It really bothers me to see one broke down on the side of the road not doing what I created it to do."

If you ever feel broken down and on the side of the road not doing what you were created to do, take heart; God plans to get you back up and on His road again. There is a great purpose for you. Consider it, know it, commit to it, then live it out – every day in a way that would cause your Father in Heaven to say, "Well done good and faithful servant. You have been faithful with a few things; I will put you in charge of many things. Come and share your master's happiness." Matthew 25:23

Bible Verse:

1 Corinthians 13:13 – "'And now these three things remain: faith, hope and love. But the greatest of these is love."

Prayer:

Lord Jesus, Thank you for loving me always, even when I fail. Thank you for loving me when I am not lovable. Thank you for forgiving me and saving me. I ask that you help me know and live the purpose you have for me. Help me to love those around me with your true love. In Jesus' name. Amen.

Take Action:

1. Write out your life purpose, mission, and vision statements. For help on this, go to www.madetochangetheworld.com/ resources and look for the *Directions for Life* book.
2. Once you draft your statements, quote them each morning for a week and adjust accordingly.
3. Commit your statements to memory and use them daily.

Additional Resources:

Book - *The Purpose Driven Life* – By Rick Warren

Movie – *The Lion King* – By Walt Disney Pictures

Music – "Jesus Take the Wheel" – By Carrie Underwood

Tool – *Directions for Life Workbook* – www.madetochangetheworld.com/resources

CHAPTER 3
THINK BIGGER

C hapter Focus: *Chapter three is about one thing: Truth. We can base our lives on many things, but the only right thing to base it on is truth. Jesus said that "you will be able to know the truth and the truth will set you free" (John 8:32). The problem is that most people are not set free today but feel in bondage. This chapter will not only help you know the truth, but will start showing you how to live by it. It will challenge your current beliefs to make sure they are based on truth. As a mentor of mine once said, "Belief is not truth. Truth is truth. Just because you believe something does not mean it is true." We will talk all about truth: what truth is, what it is not, where it comes from, and how to live by it.*

MORE IMPORTANT

There is a great story about a man who was walking on the beach one day with his grandson. There were thousands of starfish left lying on the sand when the tide went out. Unfortunately, they would not survive long in that situation. As the two walked together, the grandfather periodically picked up a starfish and threw it into the water. The little boy noticed what his grandfather was doing, surveyed the magnitude of the number of starfish onshore, then wondered what difference it would make to throw a few back into the ocean. The young child asked his grandfather, "Why are you wasting your time throwing back a couple of starfish when there are so many left? What difference does it make?" The grandpa stopped for a minute, picked up another starfish and said to his grandson, "For this starfish, it makes all the difference in the world," then threw it back into the ocean.

When it comes to starfish, they need the ocean to survive. Being out of the saltwater, away from rocks, and separated from mollusks to eat, they are doomed. Being able to put even one starfish back to where it can live and thrive is life-changing for the fish and purposeful for the grandpa. What is life-saving for humans is love, and it is purposeful for us to give love in the way God designed, to bring life back into this world and become all that we were made to be. Like the starfish all over the beach, around you every day are hurting, helpless, and hopeless people.

You may feel like the grandson in the big picture of life when it comes to the impact you think you might have as one person in this giant world. Let's look a little deeper into this story. All the stranded starfish were going to die and there were thousands of them. The grandfather knew that he could not solve the full problem by himself, but maybe he was able to save ten or more of them. The grandfather still was making a difference in what he did and it was much better to take action than not take it.

Now imagine that hundreds or even thousands of other people walked the beach that same day because grandpa got the word out that help was needed. If each person took ten or so starfish and threw them back into the water, the problem would have been solved. It would take each person having conviction, then doing his/her part by using their resources and making an effort to be part of the answer.

You and I are designed for something great by God. He invested everything into us, including the life of His Son, Jesus so that we may have a fulfilling and impactful life here on this earth. He asks us each to invest our time, energy, and talent as he did, into the world and others around us. Saving ten starfish is an impact. Everyone saving ten starfish is a world changer.

WHAT IS THE TRUTH

In this day and age, there is so much debate about what is true and not true in life. The battle for each person to claim their own truth rages on. We can see this in the news, the media, online, and even in those around us. The problem with everyone deciding on their own truth is two-fold. The first problem is that everyone is right. Therefore, there is no way to have something acceptable as a standard or foundation for humanity to co-exist. The second problem is the opposite of problem number one which is that everyone is wrong. If everyone picks their own truth, there is no truth by its very definition, just differing opinions.

Here is an example of the truth versus belief. Let's imagine my father-in-law and I were to argue over who we believe won the Super Bowl in 2010, which amazingly was NOT the New England Patriots. We could discuss this until we both pass out from exhaustion. Since my favorite team is the Pittsburgh Steelers, I am convinced that they won the Super Bowl that year. Luis' favorite Team is the Green Bay Packers so he is adamant that they won the Lombardi trophy that year.

We each have our own truth and believe and defend it. We get heated. We even start to get defensive by standing up for what we think is right, and it may hurt our relationship. The key for both of us is that we should both seek *the* truth, not our own opinions of what the truth is, because someone did win the Super Bowl that year and there is evidence to prove it. We both need to find out who won, then we will both believe that truth and join together in the belief, whether we like the truth or not.

In case you are wondering who really did win the Super Bowl that year, I'm not telling. I'm kidding. It was neither team. My Steelers won in 2009, which is what I was getting wrong in my thinking. His Packers won the Super Bowl in 2011, the year after, and this is where his thinking was off. Close, but off. The real winner that year was the New Orleans Saints. As a side note, we never did have this argument. We may debate the best team of all time, which of course, is the Steelers, but not who won the Super Bowl in 2010.

The point of this illustration is not to clarify the winner of the Super Bowl in 2010, but to clearly state that there is truth in this world and no matter how much we wish some of it were different, or try to change the truth, it is still the truth.

This earth and all of creation got here somehow. Science seems to think there was a big bang. That may have been the case because, as Rick Warren says, "If there was a big bang, there had to be a big banger." The truth of the matter is that the earth started somehow and we can make up all sorts of opinions about it and one day, after we die, we may be shown the instant replay by God to see what happened. Then we will all know the truth and have to believe it, whether we like it or not.

The more significant challenge between proving truth between a Super Bowl winner and other things like how the earth was created, if Jesus is still alive, if God really exists, etc. is that we saw the Super Bowl with our own eyes and can re-watch the game and verify the score on the ESPN app. However, God, who is invisible to our eyes, does not audibly speak to our ears. He does not show us instant replays from heaven.

In order for you to live a purposeful life full of adventure and impact, you have to decide if you believe the Bible and everything that is written in it to be true or not. We cannot pick and choose what truth is. You can choose to believe whatever you would like, but you cannot shift or make up the truth.

Just as Jesus asked Peter to come with Him to change the world, Peter had to decide if he was ready and willing to do it. He had to determine if Jesus told the truth and was someone worth following. Thankfully, he said yes, and the rest, as they say, is history. If you want to change the world in a way you cannot even imagine, you have to start with finding the truth.

THE ONE QUESTION

I was recently able to spend several days with brilliant minds in the Life Coaching industry. Many of these experts started in coaching from the very beginning more than 25 years ago when Thomas Leonard came up with the first concept. Most of these coaches have written books, spoken publicly, and worked directly with the leaders of our companies and even our country. They are the best of the best, and most hold very different beliefs about God and life than I do.

This group of top coaches are the elite experts and are impacting the world, but not generally in the way Christians would. They help people decide their direction in life without giving any thought to their creator. We each have an impact in this world, whether we want to or not; the big question is: is it in the way God desires? Is your life bringing hope and saving others, like putting the starfish back into the ocean, or is it something different? The very foundation for you to change this world must first be built on the foundation of the world itself.

While at the conference, I wondered why this wise and experienced group could not find the truth and think about God amid so many philosophies, religions, and personal desires. Then it hit me. There is only one question each of us needs to answer to determine what we will believe in life and if we will help change the world for God's purpose.

The foundational question is: "Do you believe Jesus is alive today?" Nearly everyone and all other religions believe Jesus lived. Many even believe He did great things and performed miracles. Most people think He was a great prophet and had much wisdom to offer. However, if Jesus did all these things, died, and came back to life three days later, then He really must be the Son of God and He did change the world!

There are hundreds if not thousands of prophets and wise people we could look to through history to base our hope and future on, including Muhammad and Buddha. However, all of these leading men and women have since died (or will die if still living). They could not save themselves from death. This is not to take away from some of the wisdom they had for life. Ultimately, they could not save themselves, so you cannot trust that they will save you or anyone else for the after-life.

The only "prophet" who died, was three days in the grave, then rose again to life is Jesus (according to the Bible and hundreds of historical witnesses). If He is the only one who is still alive today after overcoming death, then He is the only one we can trust with our lives on earth and for eternity. The question then becomes for each of us, "Do I believe Jesus is alive?"

Based on your answer, your future then becomes simple. If you do not believe that Jesus either existed or that He rose from the dead, then you are free to pick whatever "truth" or prophet you want to follow because they all ended up in the same place – six feet under the ground. The belief you choose will determine the extent of your impact on this world. If, however, Jesus did rise and is alive today, then your only option is to believe Jesus to be who He claims to be (the Son of God) and what is taught in the Bible.

For those of you who do believe that Jesus is the son of God and is alive today, it is time to discuss the truth He has for your life. If you don't believe Jesus is who He said He is, then you have something to consider first. Your next question to ask yourself is what (or whom) you want to put your trust and hope in for your future. From there, you can determine where you want to go with your life and who you want to follow. There have been plenty of wise people who lived throughout history and many others who are alive today. At the end of your life, you will end up where they are, but on this earth you will at least have someone or something to follow.

Incidentally, there was a top Chicago Tribune reporter years ago who not only didn't believe Jesus rose again, but also set out to disprove it in a way that only a journalist could. He researched the topic to the core over many years with great passion. If you struggle with deciding if Jesus was who He said He was and is alive today, Lee Strobel's book is a great place to start. You can read the book or even watch the movie of his life called "The Case for Christ".

If you are still undecided, I refer to a couple of other books above that would be better to start with including one of my own called "Am I Saved?," which you can find for free on the website www. madetochangetheworld.com. This book is written assuming you believe that Jesus is alive, that He is the Son of God, and that you have asked Him into your heart. The rest does not matter, including your history or your current level of faith. It's time to dive deep into the truth – about you!

Notice I didn't title this chapter "What do you believe?" because you cannot choose to believe or disbelieve something until you know what is being proposed. Let's start with the Bible, God's Word, to see if you know the core truth. In the following chapters, we will then go into what it means to believe the truth then literally live by it.

THE TRUTH ABOUT YOUR FUTURE

This world is full of influences. You can watch a great motivational speaker and feel like you can change the world. You could also watch a TV show and feel like you could never live up to what is important in this world. So where do you set your sights? What is the truth about who you are and what you should be living for? What is your purpose?

When I was fresh out of college, I had the dream to move to Florida from Ohio to be happy. I moved to Clearwater with my best friend from High School and gave it a shot. I ended up living just miles from the beach and was able to secure an excellent job as an internal auditor for a large brokerage firm. I began to establish myself in the very things I had hoped for, and yet, I was miserable! I was so miserable I found myself one day looking at the ocean and contemplating taking drugs or even killing myself.

I was doing the things I thought would make me happy and fulfilled and it didn't work. I was the opposite of happy and fulfilled. Motivational people only got me so far, and for that matter, the same applied to Pastors. I was already "religious", but that didn't help. I needed something else. Something real. Something that went to the core of who I was and gave me purpose. In all the places I searched, I couldn't find it. I ended up desperate and at the end of my rope--almost literally.

LET'S TALK ABOUT YOU NOW. YOUR LIFE. YOUR HOPE. YOUR FUTURE.

Everything that follows will be based on what the Bible says, because after all my desperate searching, the only place I found truth and answers to life was (and still is) the Bible. God and His Word are the ONLY things you need in this life and for eternity. If you are searching for anything else to fulfill you or make you happy, you are going in the wrong direction. If you are looking for any bigger purpose and impact in life than finding and following God's truth, you will not find it. As you read on, consider the following truths for your life. Your future life and ability to help change this world will depend on the foundation on which you choose to base your life.

Truth 1 – **God formed you.**

Psalm 139:13 (NLT) – "You made all the delicate, inner parts of my body and knit me together in my mother's womb"

Truth 2 – **God knows you.**

John 10:14 (ESV) – "I am the good shepherd. I know my own and my own know me."

Truth 3 – **God loves you!**

Romans 5:8 (NIV) – "God shows His love for us in that while we were still sinners, Christ died for us."

Truth 4 – **God has a plan for you.**

Jeremiah 29:11 (NIV) – "' For I know the plans I have for you', declares the Lord, 'plans to prosper you and not to harm you. Plans to give you hope and a future."

These first four truths are essential for your life. Look at each one of these and decide in your heart and mind if you believe them. If you do not believe these things, moving on to what is next in this book will not matter and here is why.

The battle for your life, your faith and your eternity relies on two things:

The first is God. If there is a God who made you, knows you, loves you, and has a plan for your life, then there is great hope and excitement for what is to come. If the Word of God is not valid, then there is no great purpose or hope for life.

The second is you. You have free will to believe and accept whatever you would like. You can make your own decisions, choose what you think is right, and base your life on just about anything. God will not stop you. He created you not to force Himself on you, but to let you choose to love and accept Him or not.

Before you move on in this book, you have to decide if you believe the first four truths. That decision will determine everything else for the rest of your life. If you do not genuinely believe in your heart and mind that the first four are correct, you should take time to ponder them and determine what you think about your origin, your value, and who God is. Moving on to the next section will mean nothing until you settle the core truths in your heart and mind.

Truth 5 – YOU must choose to serve the Lord (or not).

Joshua 24:15 (KJV) – "Choose you this day whom you will serve."

To me, the most fantastic thing about God is that He loves us so much that He lets us decide if you want to love Him back. Fake love pushes itself on another person. Real love allows the other person to make his/her own decisions, which is exactly what God does.

Before we can discuss the exciting plans God has in store for you and how to live those out, you have to make a choice. Even if you have made this choice before, I would like you to say this prayer if you are deciding to choose God!

Pray: Lord God, Father, Son, and Holy Spirit, I believe in You. I believe that You made me, that you know me, and that you love me. Thank you, Jesus, for coming to this earth, for living a perfect life and then dying for me. I believe you are alive right now. Please forgive me for all the wrong I have done and enter my heart. I believe you have a plan for me. I will seek to know you and do whatever you ask me to do. In Jesus' name. Amen.

If you prayed that prayer with sincerity of heart, God heard you. He forgave you. He will lead you. You may also want to re-pray that prayer whenever you start noticing you are slipping on the core belief of who God is and who He made you to be. It does not mean you need to be "re-saved," but it is a way to remember your commitment to and belief in God.

The following are the truths about God's power and plan for your future:

Truth 6 – **You are God's workmanship.**

Ephesians 2:10 (MSG) – "He creates each of us by Christ Jesus to join Him in the work He does, the good work he has gotten ready for us to do, work we had better be doing."

Truth 7 – **You have the power of God at work in you.**

Ephesians 3:20 (NIV) – "Now to Him who is able to do immeasurably more than all we ask or imagine, according to His power that is at work within us."

Truth 8 – **You must have faith.**

Hebrews 11:6a (AMP) – "But without faith it is impossible to (walk with God and) please Him…"

What is faith? This word is thrown around quite a bit in Christian circles, in the media, and all over the world. Because this word is so important and powerful for your life, the next chapter is focused on what it is and how to have more of it in your life to really know God and see Him work through you in mighty ways.

Here is the basis of what faith is. This is how the Bible defines faith in Hebrews 11:1 (NIV): "Now faith is confidence in what we hope for and assurance of what we do not see." God set up faith to work in this world regardless of whether you believe in Him or not. That may sound like a strange statement, but faith is like gravity and is one of the laws God established on this earth. You can believe in things and act on them before you see them, such as believing a ladder will hold you as you climb it. We must have faith in everything we do to take action.

The question becomes: where do you place your faith for your life and eternity? The answer is really simple to find out. It is based on what you think, how you spend your time, how you spend your money, and what you do with your talents. There is a whole section on this coming up next, but one keyword to point out in the definition of faith above is the word "confidence". If you want to have confidence in life and in everything you do, faith is the answer.

Truth 9 – **You must grow and mature.**

2 Peter 1:5-8 (NIV) – "For this very reason, make every effort to add to your faith goodness; and to goodness, knowledge; and to knowledge, self-control; and to self-control, perseverance; and to perseverance, godliness; and to godliness, mutual affection; and to mutual affection, love. For if you possess these qualities in increasing measure, they will keep you from being ineffective and unproductive in your knowledge of the Lord Jesus Christ."

This truth is subtle but powerful. It sounds simple, but it is difficult. It also seems minor, but is life-changing. Here is why. For most people, the first three steps are generally easy. To have the faith to believe who Jesus is and, to realize what He did for us, and to ask Him into our lives is not too hard of a step for most people. It is also usually not too difficult to be a basically good person and to have a caring and loving heart to help others. The third step is also usually easy, especially in the US, which is to gain more knowledge of God by going to church, joining a small group, or even watching Christian teachings online to grow in knowledge.

The fourth step gets harder. This is the step where many Christians fall backward and keep going back to square one and never really mature. This step in the process is self-control. Many people who accept Jesus into their hearts expect that immediately all their troubles will go away, they will automatically become Godly, and everything will change for the good. This assumption would be correct if right when you accepted Jesus into your heart, you were immediately swept up into heaven, but that is not the case. After we receive Jesus into our hearts, He allows us to remain here on this broken planet called Earth so we can learn to hear His voice, grow to be more like Him, and help others who are lost find the true hope for the world.

This means that you have to make decisions to change the way you think, what you do, and how you act based on God's promises and God's truth. He does not just jump into your brain and force you to live in a new way – it is a daily and moment by moment choice you have to make and it is not always easy. There is a constant pull to think and do things based on the world's values vs. the way God calls us to think and live. Where these two agendas hit in your life become the decision points you make in your mind, and to choose God's best in everything is called "self-control".

The fifth step can be even tougher, which is perseverance. No one likes to hear this word because it automatically stirs up negative emotions, but it does not have to do that for Christians. The *Merriam-Webster Dictionary* defines perseverance as "Continued effort to do or achieve something despite difficulties, failure, or opposition." Our world today teaches that struggle is bad and everything should be easy. This is not true! Every good thing that has been achieved in life has taken hard work, struggle, and growth – and is entirely worth it!

There is more to come in later chapters about what self-control and perseverance are and how to live these out in real life. Without them, you will never thrive and grow as God desires you to do in this life.

Truth 10 – **You will do greater things as you follow Jesus.**

John 14:12 (NIV) – "Very truly I tell you, whoever believes in me will do the works I have been doing and they will do even greater things than these because I am going to the Father. And I will do whatever you ask in my name so that the Father may be glorified through the Son."

There is a promise Jesus gave to all of us, which is that when we seek Him, and ask, and have faith, He will do even greater works through us than we read about in the Bible. What does that mean? Does that mean we can speak to thousands, heal others, and see miracles? Only God knows what He will do through you when you follow Him. That is the adventure we will discuss later in this book--the adventure that not only changes you, but impacts the world around you. That is the premise of this book. That is the premise of the Bible--the very Word of God.

CONSIDER 8TH GRADE SCIENCE

Here is something to consider from my 8th-grade science teacher using logic to explain his thinking about God and the Bible. He said that He believed in God and that he feels science continues to prove God's existence. He also believed the Bible is the accurate truth about God and tries to live by that.

He also said he could be wrong in his beliefs and one day die only to realize his belief was off. He reasoned that if that was the case and he was wrong that he lost absolutely nothing by living a Godly life based on the Bible and had more love, peace, and purpose in life than he would have had without it. However, he then reasoned that if he chose not to believe in God and the Bible to do his own thing in life and he is wrong in that decision, it would have a terrible consequence both on earth and for eternity. In his eyes, living for God was a no-lose situation.

As a good friend of mine named Erik Landvik, author of *Uncluttered Faith,* points out, my teacher was using what is commonly called "Pascal's Wager" which is "The argument that it is in one's own best interest to behave as if God exists, since the possibility of eternal punishment in hell outweighs any advantage in believing otherwise." Blaise Pascal (1623–62), who came up with this theory, was a seventeenth-century French philosopher, mathematician, and physicist. He was a brilliant, Godly man and his theory led to other theories used commonly today, such as probability theories. More important is a quote that he made after his famous theory, which is, "There is a God-shaped vacuum in the heart of each man which cannot be satisfied by any created thing but only by God the Creator, made known through Jesus Christ."

Here is the definition of truth by the *Merriam-Webster Dictionary*, which is, "The body of real things, events and facts. Actuality." What you have to decide now for yourself is what you believe. This includes the ten truths listed above. You are more than welcome to continue reading this book even if you don't believe in God, the Bible, that Jesus is alive, or the truths listed above, but without belief in those foundations, the rest of the book will just be words instead of a life-changing message.

SURVEY SAYS

One additional point to mention is that you may feel like you are the only Christian who struggles with some of these areas of faith and growth in life. The reality is that you are not. We all are growing in our faith and walk with God as we seek to become more like Him. Regardless of how long you have been a Christian or how intently you have worked on your faith, there is more growing to do with God. That is a good thing! That is the adventure He has planned for us--not a boring life, nor an unproductive one, but one of joy, excitement, and an impact on those around us.

I conducted a survey early in 2019 of over 125 Christians at all levels of maturity, length of time being Christians, churches attended, and even areas of the country. The main themes that came from the survey regarding Christian struggles were:

1) How to face obstacles,

2) How to know and find my purpose, and

3) How to increase my faith and overcome fear.

These will all be covered in this book, so let's dig into it.

Bible Verse:

2 TIMOTHY 2:15 – "'DO YOUR BEST TO PRESENT YOURSELF TO GOD AS ONE approved, a worker who does not need to be ashamed and who correctly handles the word of truth."

Prayer:

Lord Jesus, You are the way, the truth, and the life. No one comes to the Father except through you. I come to you and lay down my life, my thoughts, and all that I am. Show me your way and your truth. Set me free from the false beliefs in this world and help me to live by your truth alone. I surrender all to you and ask you to strip away any lies I believe. Replace them with your truth. I ask this in Jesus' name. Amen.

Take Action:

1. Go to www.madetochangetheworld.com to get a free copy of "Am I Saved?" then read through it if you question at all what salvation through Jesus is or whether or not you are saved.
2. Take time and read through each one of the ten truths and ask yourself if you believe each one of them enough to base your life on it.
3. If you struggle with any of the truths, ask Jesus to show you His truth (since He said He is the way, the truth, and the life) and guide your heart.

ADDITIONAL RESOURCES:

Book – *Talk Truth to Yourself* - By Brian Williams

Movie – *War Room* – By Kendrick Brothers Productions

Music – "The Voice of Truth" – By Mercy Me

Tool – *Talk Truth to Yourself* – www.madetochangetheworld.com/resources

CHAPTER 4
HAVE CONFIDENCE

C hapter Focus: *This chapter will help you increase your confidence as a Christian. The challenge of living by faith is a daily struggle for all of us, and this chapter will help you look at faith in a new way and live by it more confidently. Faith is not just something you have; it is something you do. You are always acting on faith or fear based on what you believe. These both can direct your actions. Having faith in the wrong thing or person will lead you to a bad result, as will following fear. It will also lead you down a path not desired by God. Having the confidence to know and follow God by faith is the only true way to live and have victory in all areas of this life. This chapter will help you do that.*

CONFIDENCE

Confidence is a word I hear consistently as a professional coach. It is also a word I hear consistently at church, at work, with friends, with family, in my neighborhood, and all around. It is supposed to be something that we, the children of God, have as part of our lives, yet it seems to elude most. Confidence can be our greatest asset and the lack of it our biggest obstacle.

We can have false confidence, such as the middle-aged woman who was in surgery for a heart attack and had a vision of God standing by her bedside. "Will I die?" she asked.

God said, "No. You have 30 more years to live." With 30 years to look forward to, she decided to make the best of it. Since she was in the hospital, she got breast implants, liposuction, tummy tuck, hair transplants, and collagen injections in her lips. She looked great! The day she was discharged, she exited the hospital with a swagger, crossed the street, and was immediately hit by an ambulance and killed. Up in heaven, she saw God.

"YOU SAID I HAD 30 MORE YEARS TO LIVE," SHE COMPLAINED.

"That's true," said God.

"So, what happened?" she asked.

God shrugged and said, "I didn't recognize you."

Hat tip to *Reader's Digest* "150 Greatest Jokes Ever."

Having confidence doesn't mean you can just do whatever you want, whenever you want, however you want, and have God's blessing to be successful. When you Google the word "confidence", it is defined as "1) the feeling or belief that one can rely on someone or something; firm trust. 2) the state of feeling certain about the truth of something. 3) a feeling of self-assurance arising from one's appreciation of one's own abilities or qualities."

When you are confident, you decide boldly, carry yourself firmly, and speak with conviction. Was Jesus confident? Matthew 7:29 (NLT) says this about Jesus: "… for He taught with real authority—quite unlike their teachers of religious law." He was confident in every situation, and His confidence came from His authority.

The word "authority" in the Bible, as written in Hebrew, means "Speaking in a fearless, candid, unconstrained, convincing, telling, forcible way." Jesus was able to speak with authority because He was the Son of God, knowing all the promises and truths of God. This world had nothing on Him, and we, His children, have that same authority in this life. The problem is that most Christians don't know it or believe it.

When you truly know who you are and whose you are, you will have confidence in the authority God has given you on this earth. Authority over the evil one who tries to destroy you and get you to believe wrong things. Authority over your thoughts and actions to do what God calls you to. You have the authority to be who you are called to be and live out His purpose in your life. This includes the ten truths listed in Chapter 3 of this book and all the other ones given to us throughout the Bible. God and His truth must be your focus to have true confidence in life.

WHAT ABOUT FAITH?

There is a word that ties directly to confidence, which is faith. Faith can be misunderstood and usually is. When someone says they have faith, many times they are saying they logically agree with something. However, that is only having partial faith. Faith is both a noun and a verb. In the ancient Greek language that the New Testament is written in, the word faith is two different words, one is a noun and one is a verb. Our english translation uses only the word faith and is used as a noun but is missing half of the original meaning. Faith is something you have, such as a belief in your mind that you hold as true. It is also something you do and act upon. This means that if you have faith, you don't just accept something as true in your mind; you act upon it. You have the confidence not only to say you believe something, but to live it.

In coaching, it is easy to help people identify their current situation, articulate what they want, and even set up a plan to act upon it. Getting them to act on it is a different story. I am sure you can even think about things in your own life that you have planned to do or change but haven't. It could have been something exciting you wanted to do or a goal you have always wanted to achieve. It could be something you wanted to fix or improve. It could even be what you feel God has called you to do, but you can't quite take the steps forward. You may fear obstacles such as time, money, or something else. Most of the time, however, the real obstacle is having the confidence to act upon what you say you believe.

Here is an example. My little one, Ellie, is three years old. She loves to be in the pool and swim, or at least attempt to swim. She also loves to jump around at home. Knowing she loves both of these things, I can have her stand on the side of the pool and ask her to jump because I am there to catch her. I have my arms out and will not let her slip.

She now has a choice. Does she believe in her mind I am there for her, that she can trust me and I will catch her, or does she not trust because of fear?

Her body will not just do its own thing and jump. She first needs to be convinced in her mind, from all of our times before, that I am her dad, I love her, and I will catch her.

Standing at the edge of the pool, seeing me, hearing my voice, and feeling nervous about what comes next, her little heart starts beating faster. Her adrenaline kicks in as she knows she now has a big decision to make. Will she go against what her body and mind are feeling to leave the ground and jump? She has to decide to trust. She will not know the result until she tries. She feels excitement and fear at the same time. This is the defining moment. Will she literally take a leap of faith into my arms or back away from the edge, giving in to what she feels, sees, and thinks?

Does any of this resonate with you in your Christian walk? Have you said you trust in God, yet have been asked by Him to do or change something which then tests your faith and requires it to be put into action? If so, you have felt these very feelings. You have seen the edge and stood there. Maybe you are there today. If not, you need to ask yourself if you do follow God, because this is a big part of the Christian journey!

Writing this book, launching a website, and producing tools for "Made to Change the World" requires faith in action. Although I am spending a lot of time and energy making these things, I have no idea what the response will be to the final products. However, I do believe God is calling me to do it. Do you think I am willing to act on faith? If you are reading this book, you have your answer.

Going back to my daughter's pool experience: If she decides to jump once, and I catch her, she will most likely do it again, and again, and again, and again. Acting on faith builds confidence. Here is an important point: When you act on faith with God in the small things, it then builds your confidence to trust following Him in bigger things.

Since many of you won't sleep until you know what my daughter decided to do, I will say that this summer is when we will test it out for the first time. What I can tell you is that little Ellie has felt fear and anxiety about several other things we have challenged her to do, such as walking into the water at the beach. It takes convincing to help her act in faith and not fear. Ultimately, she always trusts us and does it. The funny part is that she ends up liking the new thing so much that we can't get her to stop.

There is an important Bible verse that ties this all together. Hebrews chapter 11 is considered the faith chapter and talks about men and women who are spiritual heroes because they lived by faith even through much opposition. Verse one of Hebrews 11 (NIV) says, "Now faith is confidence in what we hope for, and assurance of what we do not see." The Message version of the Bible puts it this way: "The fundamental fact of existence is that this trust in God, this faith, is the firm foundation under everything that makes life worth living. It's our handle on what we can't see."

Do you want confidence in everything you do, in every decision you make, and in taking the right path for your life? It all comes down to faith. You have to believe that you have a Father who stands in the pool while you are standing on the edge and He tells you to "jump!" You cannot just say you believe. You cannot just rationalize God in your mind. You have to jump when He calls you. You have to have the confidence, based on God's promises, that He will always catch you.

Therefore, it is essential that you base your leaps of faith on God's Word and direction for your life. Blindly walking to the edge of the pool and jumping in just hoping that God is standing there to catch you is not faith; it is stupidity. Jumping by faith must follow God's leading; otherwise, it would be like Ellie jumping into the pool when I am not there to catch her. God gives wisdom when you ask. He gives the wisdom to know His truth, hear His voice, and follow His lead. Don't play God and presume He will do whatever you want, then act on blind faith. I will cover later in this book more of how to know it is God leading you to walk in faith by following His purpose alone.

FEAR

The opposite of faith is fear. Fear is faith in reverse. Fear is still a belief and action (or non-action) just as faith is. With fear, you believe something enough that it keeps you from taking action. You back away instead of taking the action you want to take.

We all struggle with fear in this life. You may have heard that there are various types of fears. Fear of failure, fear of heights, and fear of public speaking are just a few. Joyce Meyers has a different perspective and believes there is only one fear. The fear of pain. This could mean physical pain, emotional pain, the pain of embarrassment, etc. Instead of confidence, fear is "un-confidence" and thinking about avoiding a negative result instead of receiving a positive one.

It is wrong to believe there should be no fear in life. God wired us to have a place for fear, as well as faith. For instance, babies are born with a fear of (or reaction to) loud noises and falling. There are triggered fears that protect us and raise our senses to survey the situation and make wise decisions.

I will never forget a day many years ago that made the hair of my arms stand on end. When Claudia and I were first dating, we were part of a young adult group at church. We decided to put together a prayer list for everyone to use. At that time, neither of us had our own computer, so my boss said we could use the office computers to write, then print our prayer list.

One Friday evening, we worked on this project. Claudia was in one part of the office, and I was in the other when suddenly we both felt something. She came rushing over and asked if I felt like someone or something else was in the building. We both felt the same thing. The hair on my arms stood on end, and maybe yours is, too, as you read this.

It was a feeling, a warning that we needed to do something about. Ironically, we were working on the prayer project, so we began to pray. We also started singing some Bible hymns, and after a minute or two that feeling went away. We never did see anything, but in the pit of our souls we felt like someone, or something, was right around the corner.

That is a very spiritual example, and it gives credence to the fact that God has given us a sense of fear for a purpose. The fight or flight fear is one that helps guard us and should push us closer to God when it arises. We may have a sense of fear, yet we should always still respond in faith. Romans 14:23 says that "anything not done in faith is sin", which means we are not to live our life driven by fear.

There is one fear that we are supposed to have in life, which is the fear of the Lord. The Bible says in Proverbs 9:10 (KJV), "The fear of the Lord is the beginning of wisdom." If you do not fear the one thing you should--the Lord--then you will miss His wisdom and plan for your life.

To take this one step further, when you take seriously the meaning of life and who God is, you have a choice to make. You can accept God and His love, or you can reject Him. If you choose God, then you choose faith, which means you choose to love. Here is what the Bible says about faith and love versus fear. 1 John 4:18 (NIV) "There is no fear in love. But perfect love drives out fear because fear has to do with punishment. The one who fears is not made perfect in love." One additional verse to support this truth is 1 John 4:8 (NIV) "...God is love."

When you are living in love, or in God, there is no fear because you are close to Him. You know Him, and He knows you. You feel His love and forgiveness, and you do not fear punishment but have confidence in what you believe. This relationship of being close with your Father, who is the creator of the universe and who loves you, removes fear. Ultimately your focus then is on God and not the things of this world. This is true faith and confidence.

To use my daughter as an example again, I can see this concept at work in her as her earthly father. When I am close to her she is very confident in herself and what she is doing. When I am not around, she begins to look for me (or her mother) and look for safety. She will play comfortably for hours when she knows we are nearby and she feels she can come to us at any time. The boundaries we set, although sometimes frustrating to her, make her feel secure.

Some nights Ellie says she is afraid. Afraid of the dark, fearful of noises, or something similar. When she comes to me in fear, I pick her up and hold her. I explain that I am here and there is nothing to fear. Sometimes I turn on the light or investigate a sound to show her there is nothing to fear. I hold her. I pray with her. I confirm that I am close by and nothing will harm her. She has peace and goes on playing or returns to bed because she knows her father is there, and she trusts me.

When you walk closely with God, your heavenly Father, He affirms you. He affirms that He loves you. He is there for you, and He will protect you. He affirms the direction He would have you take in life. He will be there every step along the way. God also affirms the steps He would like you to take by faith. In this relationship, there is no room for fear because this perfect love of our eternal Father drives it out.

Ultimately the deciding factor between faith and fear is trust. If you put your complete trust in your heavenly Father, you will live by faith. If you place your trust in anything or anyone else (including yourself) you will live by a combination of faith and fear.

Here is where the rubber meets the road. Anyone can say he is a Christian and believe in God. It is not hard to make that claim. It is quite another thing to fully trust God with absolutely every area of your life and act with complete assurance and certainty on the things you hope for and do not see, simply because God asks you to.

One important note: one thing that can trip you up is that you could give in to the fear that if you do something by following God, you will fail. Here is another key truth for you to remember: If you do what you feel God is calling you to do in faith, you cannot fail. Here is why. God directs us to live by faith but not to control the outcome. Only He has control of the outcome. Only God knows what the result will be of you walking in faith, and it may be very different from what you expect. Sometimes the result may seem like a failure, but there is a holy victory that you don't see-- or perhaps don't see yet. Choose faith and focus on following, then trust the outcome to God.

As a side note, as you are learning to hear and follow God more closely, inevitably there will be a time when you think it is God and do something on faith, only to realize it wasn't God's leading. That is okay. That is how you learn. As long as you are seeking God, applying His Word, and acting on faith, He will teach you more and more to hear His voice. Any mistakes you make by trying to follow Him, He will work for good. (Romans 8:28-30).

My sister Stephanie is now living in Thailand with her husband and three daughters. It doesn't make sense. They do not know the culture or language. Thailand is considered one of the most unchurched nations in the world. It is not the safest place for kids, especially with all the human trafficking coming out of Bangkok. So, why are they there? Because God called them to be there. Against better judgment, against other recommendations, against feelings and emotions, they are living by faith and not fear. They are learning a language and a culture so they can be a light in the dark world of Thailand and bring the good news of Jesus Christ to them.

Many people fear that by fully following God, they will be called to do scary things, such as being called to be a missionary to a foreign land. Don't let this hold you back from fully committing to God. Don't worry--I felt that same apprehension, but God did not call me to the foreign mission field, nor does He call the majority of Christians to do that. Yes, if He does call you, He will also empower you to do His will.

We will cover later in the book how to know if it is God calling you to do something by faith or if the thought is coming from yourself, others, or even the evil one. The one last thing I will add is that when you begin to feel fear, surrender it to God. Get on your knees and turn everything over to Him. This means all that you have, all that you are, and all that you do. Let the results be in His hands, whatever those are, and follow in faith every day of your life.

THE POINT

For those of you old enough to remember movies from the 1980s, a movie came out in 1988 called *Indiana Jones and the Last Crusade*. Indiana ("Indie" as everyone called him) was an archaeologist who was in search of the Holy Grail. This grail was the cup Jesus drank from at the last supper. Of course, this whole movie was fiction. However, the action was fantastic.

All through the movie, while Indie was in search of his dream, he was being chased, attacked, and threatened. He never gave up, even while he faced some nerve-wracking situations including encounters with snakes, boulders, and enemy fire. He kept going until he found a secret cave and the place where an ancient soldier guarded the Holy Grail.

As Indie walked up to the soldier, he first had to fight him to get the right to find the grail that Jesus used amongst hundreds of cups. If he happened to drink from the wrong cup, it would mean instant death. As Indie went to pick up the cup, the soldier said two words that summed up Indie's huge decision and our very existence on this earth. His words were "Choose wisely." Then he said, "As the true grail will bring life, the false one will take it from you." Thankfully, Indie did choose wisely and lived, while another man didn't and instantly died.

Each day throughout your life, you have decisions to make. You can choose to pull close to God, or away from Him. Just as the movie clip describes, you are in a battle (spiritually) that takes place in your mind and your heart. Without clear beliefs, a close relationship with God, and the conviction and power of God within you, you will choose poorly. Those poor decisions lead to repercussions here on earth and possibly in eternity.

God will not make decisions for you. You must decide. God will give you wisdom, direction, strength, and guidance as you ask for it, but He will never force you to make the right decision. You are responsible for the focus of your mind. Every decision leads to action that either glorifies God or pulls you away from Him. The choice--every choice--is yours.

Here is the point. There are forces at work in our world and in our minds every day. God calls us to trust Him and walk in faith regardless of what we see and feel. Many times, this world and our senses want us to follow what we think or feel is right based on fear or our selfish desires. Don't follow these paths. As the movie says, you must make it your number one goal to focus on God and choose wisely.

HOW TO CHOOSE WISELY

If you want to follow God, you will need to make the right decisions in three key areas of life. The first deals with the things God has already clearly spelled out in His Word, the Bible. These are clear directives that should find all Christians on the same page and standing strong together. Examples include following the Ten Commandments (have no other God, don't lie, don't kill, etc.). Taking care of widows and orphans and not having sex with anyone other than your spouse also fall into this category.

The second area deals with certain sections of the Bible that may not be as clear-cut as the Ten Commandments, yet are based on your faith. God will lead you into what is right. For instance, some people believe that drinking alcohol is perfectly fine for them as Christians, while others wouldn't touch it. The Bible is clear that being drunk is a sin and that too much alcohol can lead to all sorts of trouble, while on the other hand, Jesus and the disciples drank wine. There are other areas like this through the years, such as dancing, eating certain foods, etc. that provoke conflict. For those areas where the Bible does not seem to be as clear, it is important to ask God what He requires of you. A good rule of thumb is that if there is *anything* in your life that you could not turn over to Him immediately if He asked you to, then it has become another "god" or an addiction, and that is not what God desires.

The third area deals with those life decisions we get to make that are neither sinful nor holy (as spelled out in the Bible), but are essential and require God's direction. For example, if you are offered a new job position, considering what college to attend, or are looking to move cross-country, these decisions are not obvious from the Bible, and yet God has a plan. Taking time to find the right plan is the key. I will discuss this more in later chapters.

Choosing wisely requires you to know where God clearly says yes and no. It also requires that you look at every area of your life to see if anything is too important or too strong for you to give up. Finally, choosing wisely also requires that in those less obvious decisions, you walk closely enough with God that you can see what my friend and mentor, Buddy Owens calls the "arrows" of His direction.

Here is an important reminder:

Faith (noun) – "Allegiance to duty or a person. A firm belief in something for which there is no proof. Complete trust. Something that is believed especially with strong conviction." (Miriam Webster)

Faith (verb) – "Believe, Trust". This is a transitive verb, which means "being characterized by", or in other words doing what you have faith in. (Miriam Webster)

Faith – "Now faith is confidence in what we hope for and assurance about what we do not see. (Holy Bible" – Hebrews 11:1-3).

Faith – "comes from hearing, and hearing from the Word of God."

When you firmly believe in God with complete trust and conviction, your life will be characterized by it. You will have confidence and assurance about your daily life and every step you take. This can only come from spending time with God through prayer and being in His Word each day. By doing this, you will be firm about God's truth and promises, your convictions, who you are, and what you are to do. This does not mean life will always be easy, because it won't. It does mean that you can count on God and all His promises for your life.

LUTHER

As you can tell, I like to illustrate with stories, examples, songs, and movies. Another movie to demonstrate the conviction of knowing and then living by faith is titled *Luther*. More than 500 years ago, Martin Luther was a German monk who was cut to the soul by his convictions. He did not believe the Roman Catholic Church was right to pressure people to "pay" to have their sins forgiven, nor did he believe you had to earn your way to heaven by "good works". This is well before printed Bibles were in common languages, so people had to rely on whatever the priests proclaimed.

Martin became so disgusted that he printed his own book to teach what the Bible said about salvation, grace, and faith in Jesus. In the movie, Luther stated, "It is a symbol of my intent – to restore Christ's church." He wrote his confession of faith, and was later excommunicated by the pope and condemned as an outlaw by the Holy Roman Emperor.

I point this out because Martin Luther knew what he believed, read the Bible, and prayed to God. He knew the conviction God had placed upon him, and would not turn away. A scene in the movie that forever stands in my mind depicts the night before his trial. He was confined to a tiny room, which was a jail cell type of environment. That night he was tortured in his mind and spirit by the Devil. The intensity of the situation was so strong it tempted him to turn back, to give in, and to back down from his conviction. He was facing death and had to decide if it was worth it.

Martin was sure of what he hoped for and certain of what he did not see. He stood upon the conviction God put on his heart, and as they say, the rest is history. It changed the church forever as Martin was excommunicated but continued to teach the Bible based on his conviction. Today there are many Christian denominations in the world, because of Luther's stance.

Many of us today are not in nations where living by faith in God will bring the consequences Martin Luther faced. However, we sometimes feel that tension within us to do what is right, even though we may be disliked, misunderstood, threatened, fired, or otherwise mistreated. It is sometimes emotional and stretching to live by our convictions and stand up for what is right. It can shake us to our very core. Yet, such is the path to follow God and live a life full of purpose and love. It can also be the most significant challenge we will ever face in life. That challenge is to follow by faith!

To have confidence, you must commit and take responsibility and follow through. God has already committed everything in heaven and earth for you. Now it is your turn. If you believe Jesus is alive and you believe all of God's truths, then your commitment needs to be not just to trust God in your mind, but also to act on it with every part of who you are. The result of doing so is peace, love, and joy on this earth and an even better eternity. What to commit to comes next!

I will finish this chapter with lyrics to a song titled "Dive" by Stephen Curtis Chapman:

...My heart is racing, and my feet are weak

As I walk to the edge

I know there is no turning back

Once my feet have left the ledge

And in the rush, I hear a voice

That's telling me to take a leap of faith

So here I go

I'm diving in, I'm going deep, in over my head I want to be

Caught in the rush, lost in the flow, in over my head I want to go

The river's deep, the river's wide, the river's water is alive

So sink or swim, I'm diving in

There is a supernatural power

In this mighty river's flow

It can bring the dead to life

And it can fill an empty soul

And give a heart the only thing

Worth living and worth dying for, yeah

But we will never know the awesome power

Of the grace of God

Until we let ourselves get swept away

Into this holy flood

So if you take my hand

We'll close our eyes and count to three

And take the leap of faith

Come on let's go

I'm diving in, I'm going deep, in over my head I want to be

Caught in the rush, lost in the flow, in over my head I want to go

The river's deep, the river's wide, the river's water is alive

So sink or swim, I'm diving in

Oh...Come on let's go...

When it comes to the will of God, you are in charge of the decision to follow or not. When God shows you what to do and asks you to take a leap of faith, you are responsible= for your decision and for taking action. God is responsible for the results.

Bible Verse:

James 2:17 (ASV) – "Even so faith, if it does not have works, is dead in itself."

Prayer:

Lord Jesus, increase my faith. I believe in you. Help me to follow you in all I think, say, and do.

Take Action:

1. Decide if you are ready, able, and willing to surrender every area of your life.
2. If you are ready, then pray a prayer that turns everything over to Him. If you are not ready, write the reasons why and then pray and ask God to help you want to turn those areas over to Him.

Additional Resources:

Book - *Experiencing God* by Henry and Richard Blackaby and Claude King

Movie – *Luther* by Mark Burnett and Roma Downey

Music – "Dive" by Stephen Curtis Chapman

Tool - *Walk with God Today* www. madetochangetheworld.com / resources

CHAPTER 5
BEHAVIOR CHANGE

hapter Focus: This is a critical chapter in the book, and I will even dare to say it is the most important because it is about how to make changes in your life. Until now, you have read about things that will get you to think, explore, dream, and ask God about. The main thing this book has most likely done for you so far is to get you to consider new things. As you may recall from chapter 4, faith is a noun that requires action. It is something you think, and also something you live. You probably have things you have wanted to change or do in life, maybe for a long time, and have not done them. These could even be things God has been prompting you to do. This chapter will show you how you work, then help you actually make these changes.

AWKWARD CHALLENGE

One day, a group of hot-shot scientists believed they had everything figured out. They had explored how the human body, mind, and all of its systems work. They had already cloned animals and felt they could not only do this with humans, but also they could make a human and bring it to life. They then decided to challenge God in creating a new human being from scratch.

God was more than happy to take them on in this challenge. They set the time and the date for the big event six months out. When that day came, they all gathered together to get ready to start the competition of creating a new human. Thousands of people gathered around to watch. The anticipation had everyone buzzing and on the edges of their seats.

As the starting gun was ready to sound, God called a halt to the challenge. He asked the scientists what they were going to use to make a new human. They showed him the dirt, chemicals, and all the elements they had ready to go. God then said that if they wanted to compete with him, they also needed to create all their own material to make a human. That quickly ended the competition!

LOGIC, WILL, AND EMOTIONS

God has made you a fantastic being. If you read the first two chapters of Genesis in the Bible, it describes how God made all of creation with His very Word, which is Jesus. More about that in Chapter 10. On the sixth and final day of creation, He made his most magnificent design of all – Adam and Eve. He took the elements of the earth that He had created and then formed the body of Adam. Adam was made from dirt and chemicals and was lifeless. Then God breathed His Spirit into his nostrils, and Adam came to life. No one and no modern science or technology have ever been able to duplicate this "breath of life", which is because it literally means "spirit of God".

That breath of life was breathed into mere dirt and chemicals and it made the heart, lungs, veins, and organs begin to function. The brain also began to fire with independent thoughts. What was a model of clay just minutes before, was now a thinking, breathing, and moving body.

Within that body was the first brain stem, as we call it today. It is the command center. It regulates our heartbeat, our breathing, our walking and talking, our thinking, and the very being of who we are. Modern science is still trying to fully understand the human brain and its capacity for logic, emotions, and decision-making.

How incredible you are! You are a walking miracle. You are a human being who has the very breath of God in you that enables you to think, move, and live. Within you is the capacity to learn, grow, and decide. You get to make your own decisions and think your own thoughts. God does not force you to believe a certain way. He may bring you to points of decision, but those decisions are still always up to you.

God formed us with the ability to live on three planes all at once – physical, mental and spiritual. The place where our physical, mental and spiritual worlds interact is in our minds. To really understand this, the mind itself must be broken down into its simplest components, which is best described by Jesus. In the book of Matthew, Jesus was asked what the greatest commandment was in all creation. He replied that it is to "love the Lord your God with all your heart, soul, mind, and strength." The first three relate directly to our mind, and strength relates directly to our physical body.

So what are your "heart, soul, and mind?" When looking at the Greek-- the original language in which the book of Matthew was written--the word "heart" means emotions, "soul" means will, and "mind" means logic. This is who you *really* are. You are the interaction between these three components, which causes you to think and believe the way you do in every area of life. When these three areas are operating in harmony, there is peace in your mind. When they are working against each other, there is much inner turmoil and confusion.

In general, every person has one area that is stronger or more domi-nant than the other. They all have an influence on the way you think and decisions you make, but generally, if you are an emotional person, decisions can be swayed by how you feel. If you are a logical person, your choices will be made based on whether they make sense to you. If you have a strong will, many of your decisions will be made based upon what drives you. We each have all three capacities, but at times, one pushes us more than the others.

Which one is the most important? The best way to answer the question is to think of a real-life scenario that shows how these interact in our lives. Many people have committed to lose weight or get in shape. In the first couple of weeks it is usually not too difficult to keep that commitment. Now, let's say at the beginning of week three you wake up on Monday at 6:00 A.M. and you don't FEEL (emotion) like going. The next thing you do is THINK (logic) about your alternatives and determine that you can make it up tomorrow and sleep in. In the back of your mind, you realize that you made a COMMITMENT (will) and should stick to this. Most people will give in to what they feel and rationalize. Here is the key – your will (also known as resolve, determination, or commitment) must override your logic and emotions if you are to do and be all that you dream of and desire.

The will is where faith comes from, where habits are changed, and where the conditioning of the mind takes place. When you want to change, achieve, or grow, then you must have what's called a "burning desire". Otherwise, you will not keep the commitment when you don't feel like it, but will instead rationalize it away. This is the most powerful part of who you are because it is where passion is and where the decision to do anything happens. The key for us as Christians is to continually turn over our thoughts, feelings, and desires to God so that He will put in us the things that are of Him, and help us remove everything that is not. This is a daily struggle to set our minds and thoughts on Him and not on the things we see and hear in this world, as Colossians 3:2 reminds us to do.

LEARNING VS. LIVING

You may feel like you know this or have heard some of these concepts before. We generally know what to do, but there is a big difference between knowing and doing. Here is a realistic look at the difference between learning about God and living for God.

MANY YEARS AGO, I WENT TO COLLEGE AND GOT MY ACCOUNTING DEGREE. I felt that it would be my golden ticket. I believed I would get a great job, perform exceedingly well with all my new knowledge, and have a good life. The problem came when I had to take my acquired book knowledge into the real world.

My first shock was that no one came knocking on my door to give me a job. I had to have the self-discipline to create a resume proactively, apply, interview, and hope to get a position. There was no class in school to help with this; it was something I had to learn by doing. I had to submit applications and go through the interview process, which was not comfortable in and of itself, and at times it took self-control to handle my frustrations. When I finally did get my first job in accounting, it was much different in the real world from what it was like in class.

I started in the Accounts Receivable department. That is a fancy name for "collections"! I had to call all the people who had overdue accounts and try to get them to pay their bills. Although school taught me about the debit and credit side of the books, it never taught me how to call people who were not paying, or how to collect the money so I could then write it off by debiting cash and crediting the account receivable. The book part was easy; the application was hard and took a while to figure out.

The great news is that after a year, the receivables went to almost zero after a very high starting balance. I found a way to connect with those who owed the money by hearing their stories and working with them on a payment plan they could execute. This whole process took days, weeks, and sometimes months. It also took self-control when I would get cursed out by people who didn't want to pay their bills, and self-discipline to keep trying new ways to make it work.

In your spiritual life, you can go to church or join a small group and learn all the key things about living for God. Putting them into practice in real life is a whole new challenge. It is great to read about loving your neighbor, but it is entirely different to do it when they are rude to you or their barking dog keeps you up all night! Do you become angry and verbally abusive, or do you find a way to love them the way God desires?

The Bible is not a book to read. It is a book to live. The connection with God is not a one-way street where He gives you everything regardless of what you do. It is a two-way relationship where there is communication, love, and trust, and then your thoughts and actions follow it. This life is not something to get through. Life is a blessing from God to truly live.

PHILOSOPHY OF BEHAVIOR CHANGE

I recently wrote a ten-page summary of behavior change. This comes from my nearly 20 years of ministering, coaching, and helping people grow and make changes in their lives. Because of the fantastic way God created us with our ability to think, feel, and respond, our ability to change what we believe and how we live is both incredible and difficult.

I once heard a pastor inaccurately say that the only way to change is to trust in God and let the Holy Spirit change you instead of exercising your will power. Through my many years of helping both Christians and non-Christians change in all sorts of areas, including health, finances, career, relationships, etc., I can confidently say that God designed everyone with the capacity to learn, grow, and change. The benefit that Christians have in this process is that the change is led by God and empowered by the Holy Spirit. We still have the choice to change or not – God will never force us.

Here are the basics of how we change.

In the previous section, I discussed logic, will, and emotion. Those are the exact three areas of our mind and life that cause us to change or not change. When they are all engaged, you will likely make changes in life. If just one or two of these parts of your mind are involved in that area, there is a good chance change will not happen.

The best way to explain this is with an example. Let's imagine that you are considering making the small and simple change of spending ten minutes each morning with God by reading the Bible and praying. The first thing that happens is that you learn that God wants to spend time with you and that a big key to being a Christian is your relationship with Him. Learning about this may bring something new to your mind, which is called **awareness**. You then begin to consider this new idea for a few minutes. You may even think about this over days, weeks, or even months. You might start thinking about how you could fit a ten-minute quiet time with God into your schedule.

As you spend more time thinking about it, you may notice some feelings arise. Those feelings could be stress regarding trying to find time to do this. They could be excitement about actually spending more time with God. They could even be fear of wondering if you spend time with God, what He would lead you to do. You may not even recognize that these feelings develop when you consider this change, but they are there underneath your decision-making.

At some point, you come to a **decision.** That decision is based on what you have been thinking, what you have been feeling, and your level of determination to make this change. If this is something you are very determined to do, you will push yourself mentally to find a way to do it. You will think of a time in your schedule that you can fit in ten minutes each morning. You may talk to friends or a pastor to find out how to best start doing this, or what chapter in the Bible to read. You get excited about growing close to God, and then find a day to start this. You may also go another direction and feel that this isn't that important. You decide that you do not have time to do it and that it is something you will not pursue right now.

All of these processes go on in our minds, sometimes quite rapidly, regarding all the decisions we make. This causes us to move forward, or not move forward, on something. You can apply this to almost any area of life, including getting out of debt, stopping smoking, losing weight, looking for a new job, and the list goes on. You may be thinking of something right now that you are considering changing in your life. What is that process like in your mind?

Here is the story behind the story. Generally, the first step to changing anything begins with **awareness.** For example, if I told you that a certain type of tea has been proven to heal any sickness you may have, you have just learned new information. You are now aware of what this tea can do. You will logically process this. You may quickly feel that you are not sick, so you don't need it. You may question if the information is even right. You could immediately believe it and realize what ailments this could fix. Now that you are aware of this new information, you can choose to do something with what you have learned, or you could choose to do nothing at all. However, you cannot become unaware of new information. Your mind will process what to do next.

As soon as you start thinking about what you just learned, you may become **emotional** about it. If you have been sick lately, you will probably get excited that there is a new cure for you. The more you think about it, the happier you get. In this case, your logical thinking and feelings are working together. Your mind could also go in a different direction as you analyze the new report and feel it is false because you have had green tea before and nothing happened. Now you are feeling frustrated and logically not believing any of this. Now two parts of your brain are engaged with taking in this new information. They are either in agreement with each other or not. When your logic and your emotions don't agree, that is called **ambivalence,** and it is where people get stuck in life.

Then the third area of mental functioning comes in as your will **(determination)**. Keep in mind this whole process could happen over split seconds or could be things you consider and think about for long periods. Ultimately, your will is the deciding factor. Using the tea example, you could have been feeling sick for a long time and would be willing to try anything at this point. Your logic says this could be a breakthrough, and if your emotions are hopeful, then you may confidently decide you are going to drink a gallon of this tea each day. Okay, maybe not a gallon, but you definitely are going to take action. If you are thinking and feeling the opposite, then your will is not engaged to move forward, and the decision to do this is probably "no".

Through these simple examples, you can see how amazing and complex we are as humans. Imagine, then, what goes through your mind when you have big life decisions such as making a career change, getting married, having a baby, accepting Jesus, or dealing with a family member's health issue. The reason behavior change can be so difficult is because our mind goes in many different directions, feels many different ways, and sways on its commitments.

Going back to the greatest commandment, which is to "Love the Lord our God with all our heart, soul, mind, and strength", the Scripture is saying that we have to make a complete decision of the will to follow God. Sometimes this commitment to God will have to override your logic and your emotions. You may have times when God is leading you to do something that doesn't seem to make sense or you don't feel confident about, and you will have to determine if you will stick to your commitment to God and act on faith.

Here is another example of how our minds work in situations of faith. Let's say you are in church on Sunday and the Pastor quotes scripture about forgiveness. He states that if you don't forgive others, then God won't forgive you. Immediately, you think of someone in your life you are mad at. You may have been holding a grudge, and now you hear that you must forgive them. The same process described above starts. You take in the information, you get emotional or even mad about the situation with this person and your first inclination is to decide you will not forgive them. However, the challenge now is that you have already committed to God to follow Him. There is now a battle within you to either follow your desire to continue in bitterness and resentment because you were wronged, or to go against your internal thoughts and feelings to do what God is asking you to do.

You can probably think of many areas this would apply to in your life and walk of faith. You may have had this exact situation occur, or something similar where you are feeling one thing, yet God through His Word is saying to do another. This then becomes your decision-making time, and God will never force you to do it His way, but He will lead you to many places where you have to choose. This has been the case since day one on earth. Unfortunately, that first couple, Adam and Eve, got to a point where they decided to go against what God said and to follow their thoughts, feelings, and wills. All of creation has been paying for it ever since.

The summary of behavior change philosophy looks like this:

1. You become aware of something

2. It first hits your logical thinking (either briefly or for a long time)
3. It can then turn into something emotional, which is deeper
4. Your will kicks in and causes you to take action (or not take action)

HOW TO CHANGE

The philosophy is easy to understand, but how does that help you with actually making changes in your life? In the late 1970s, James Prochaska and Carlo Di Clemente conducted a study in which they were trying to help smokers quit smoking. Their *Transtheoretical Model* suggests that people go through six stages as they change. Important points to consider here are that change is not linear (meaning doesn't always happen precisely in sequence) nor is there a good or bad stage. It merely describes what people are thinking and doing as they decide to change or not. Here are the stages from the summary on Wikipedia (with slight modifications based on ways I have trained it):

- Pre-contemplation ("I won't change") – "People are not intending to take action in the foreseeable future, and can be unaware that their behavior is problematic."
- Contemplation ("I might change") – "People are beginning to recognize that their behavior is problematic, and start to look at the pros and cons of their continued actions."
- Preparation ("I will change") – "People are intending to take action in the immediate future, and may begin taking small steps toward behavior change."
- Action ("I am changing") – "People have made specific overt modifications in modifying their problematic behavior or in acquiring new healthy behaviors."
- Maintenance ("I have changed") – "People have been able to sustain an action for at least six months and are working to prevent relapse."
- Termination – Individuals have zero temptation and they are

sure they will not return to their old unhealthy habit as a way of coping. As a side note, even though "Termination" is listed here, I do not believe that during this life on earth this is ever really going to happen because of our continuing battle with sin and the evil one.

One highlight to note here is that although this study was conducted with smokers, it applies to all areas of life-change. The second key point is that all of these stages carry with them what we discussed earlier regarding your logic, emotions, and will. Finally, some things can help each of these stages progress. For example, if you are in the first two stages in a certain area of life, continuing to learn more about that area can increase your desire to do it. Additionally, in "Preparation", a well-thought-out plan can help you be successful. Finally, in "Action" and "Maintenance", accountability and close support go a long way toward ensuring a successful outcome.

Incidentally, this is why coaching, counseling, discipleships, and small groups can have a tremendous impact on helping people change. For more on coaching, go to madetochangetheworld.com / coaching.

The most important thing to understand here is that when we are going to make a change in anything in life, it is not a simple process. God and the Holy Spirit will help us through any change He is asking us to make. Ultimately the choice to change is up to us, and with God's power and strength, we can do anything He asks us to do.

Interestingly, Zig Ziglar simplifies this whole process in our mind by saying that people change for one of two reasons: "inspiration or desperation." It has also been stated that when the pain of staying the same outweighs the pain of making the change, we will decide to make the change. As Christians, we should always be willing to seek, find, and follow God in whatever He asks us to do. Fortunately (or unfortunately), we have to deal with our logic, emotions, and will to get there. Not only that, we have a world around us telling us to do the opposite many times, and an enemy, the Devil, who will try to get us to do anything other than God's will.

So, to give you one final analogy to help you with this, I am going to use a funny cartoon about *Bugs Bunny*. Ralph E. Wolf's job in life was to try to get an unsuspecting sheep for his dinner, and Sam the Sheepdog's job was to protect the sheep. Ralph would continuously come up with these schemes to get to the sheep, and Sam would have to be sharper than Ralph and catch him at his games. It became quite funny at times because when it would look like Ralph finally found some prey, Sam would jump in and save the day! Some of you are old enough to remember this, and if you're not, I am sure you are Googling it now.

Imagine now that in your mind, you are Sam the sheepdog, and continuously coming around you is Ralph the Wolf. As the sheepdog, you have all the sheep in a pen that is surrounded by a fence. You guard the fence always to see what or who is trying to get in. When the sheepherder or farmer comes around you let him right in. But when anyone else comes to the gate, you have to be very conscious of who it is and whether or not you should let him or her in.

That gate is your logical mind. It has things approaching it all the time. The world will present many thoughts to you, God will lead you with ideas, and the evil one will try to do what he does best – deceive you! Just like Sam the Sheepdog, you have to know for what and for whom to open the gate. The only real way you can do this as a Christian is to know God's Word and to not allow thoughts and ideas that oppose the truth to come into your mind. Whenever you gauge ideas that come to your mind by anything other than God's Word, you have a real risk of letting in the enemy.

The pen where the sheep are held is comparable to your emotions. Once you let a thought enter the gate and dwell in your mind, it starts to reach your heart. When that idea or person is from God, it will increase your faith, develop the fruit of the Spirit, and lead you. When it is from the enemy, it will bring fear, worry, or doubt. What you allow through the gate could be a direct temptation to sin. The enemy at the gate always brings lies and deception, and if you don't ask God and the Holy Spirit to help you discern right and wrong, you will quickly allow the wrong thing. Once that evil thought gets into the "pen", you start to become very emotional. Good things bring in the fruit of the spirit such as "love, joy, peace, patience, kindness, goodness, faithfulness, gentleness, and self-control," Galatians 5:22-23. When you let in the wrong things, it leads to great stress and adversity within your heart, because "the enemy comes to kill, steal, and destroy," John 10:10.

The very things you continually let into your mind and heart (emotions) are the same things that will, over time, drive your will and decisions. If the very center of your will (that guards the sheep) is to follow God, you will need to defend your thoughts and heart with the truth of His Word and keep out the things that are not of Him. This all relates to change, because it comes down to your decision-making and commitments.

DECIDING TO COMMIT

Every day, many things hit your heart and mind. You have to make decisions constantly. Some decisions are simple, and some can be life-changing. When it comes to behavior change and intentionally doing or thinking something new in life, there comes the point where you have to decide and then commit. *A decision without a commitment is a decision not to do it.* I could say I am going to start tracking my spending, but if I don't make a clear commitment with a set plan and support in place, I will not do it.

Commitment, defined by Miriam Webster's Dictionary is defined as, "an agreement or pledge to do something in the future; an engagement to assume a financial obligation at a future date; something pledged, the state or an instance of being obligated or emotionally impelled; an act of committing to a charge or trust."

Consider the time you asked Jesus into your heart. If you have not done this, I recommend reading "Am I Saved?" by going to www.madetochangetheworld.com/resources. At the time you heard about who Jesus was and what He did for you, you probably began to think about it, consider it, then even feel things emotionally. You had to get to the place to make a big decision based on your will and desire, which was to be forgiven, to know God, and follow Him. You then would have committed to saying a prayer and asking Jesus into your heart. That decision caused you to speak words of surrender to Jesus, commit your life to Him, and follow as best you could. Hopefully, that relationship has changed your life. You have probably heard it said of someone who accepts Christ that the person "committed his/her life to Jesus."

The challenge that happens after the commitment can be summed up in three simple words: "What is next?" Without a plan or next steps, it makes a commitment merely words. Taking the earlier example of accepting Christ, the next steps should be along the lines of spending time with God, spending time with other Christians, and/or getting involved in some studies. Without application, a commitment won't turn into behavior change.

A second key to commitment is supportive accountability. This is not about judging. It is about partnering to help someone move in the direction in which they feel led. That relationship is based on love and caring, and the support person is able to ask direct questions, share observations, and help the other person fulfill his/her commitment. This is one reason why I love coaching and the coaching process. Done right, it provides a partner who is a complete ally who stands for you and your areas of growth, even in times when you may not feel like standing for yourself. This also can apply to Godly friendships, mentoring, discipleship, ministry, small groups, and counseling, among other Godly type relationships.

Here is how the steps to change generally work:

1. Awareness – This is the first step to change. Until you are aware of something, you can't even decide if you want to change it. Once you are aware, you cannot become unaware of that thing. You may already know of an area of your life God wants you to change.

2. Decision – Based on your new awareness and understanding, you have to decide if you believe it, and also if you want to act on it. The choice is still yours. If God shows you something to pursue, change, or act upon, He is not automatically going to

change it for you. He will never force you to do anything. You
now have to decide if you will take action and commit to it.

3. Plan – If you feel there is something God wants you to pursue,
change, or do differently, you must make a plan of action of
how and when to do it. It may be something you will do
immediately, or it may take longer. Depending on the area you
are going to be working on, there are many ways to set goals.
Many people are familiar with SMART goals. Rick Warren's
acronym of "FAITH" is another way to help you formulate a
goal.

F - Focused (specific) – You must have a clear, not vague, goal

A - Attainable (achievable) – You must believe it in faith, or don't set
the goal

I - Individual (for you) – Only set a goal for you, not someone else

T - Trackable (measurable) – Be able to track it and prove you did it

H - Heartfelt (passionate) – You must be passionate, or it won't happen

4. Execution – Make the change. Sometimes this is easy and sometimes
it's difficult. The goal may include changing long term habits and ways
of thinking as you move forward, and this can take time and effort.
The most important thing to know is that as a Christian, you are not on
your own; God will help you! The Holy Spirit is your strength and
your power. You will overcome.

5. Accountability – Who will know if you are keeping your commitments? God does – all the time. He can and will help you. It is also
essential to have a Christian brother or sister to support you, and in
whom you can confide. The best way to do this is with Christian
support such as a pastor, a Christian relative or friend, a mentor, a
small group, or even a coach. If a Christian coach is a direction of
interest to you, go to www.madetochangetheworld.com to find one.

Something important to know and remember when following God's plan for your life is Proverbs 16:9 – "In his heart, a man plans his course, but the Lord determines his steps." This means that you seek God to set the plans He puts on your heart, work toward your commitment, and always be open to how He leads you along that path; don't just get set in your own way.

Here is an example of how God did that with me many years ago. He had put in my mind the idea of developing a new Christian financial training program. I started researching it, coming up with ideas, and putting it together. A couple of weeks into my life's new direction, I called my church and they put me in touch with a financial advisor who had volunteered to help people with their money situations. I went to meet with him at his business, which was a partnership with two other Christian men in financial planning. We had a great meeting. Even more than that, we had a God encounter. I never actually started that business, but I did end up going to work for Kip, the volunteer, and his company for over four years!

My friend and mentor, Buddy Owens, says, "Follow the arrows" as God leads you through His plan for your life. As a follower of Jesus, you should not leave your life up to chance and hope God does everything for you with no action on your behalf. At the same time, getting stuck on your plan and your goals can take you way off course. Set the plan you feel God is directing, then follow by faith as He changes or adjusts the direction to get you to your destination.

You may already have something that comes to your mind for which to plan. God may also use the next couple of chapters to show you things to set plans for in your life. If you are setting a goal and making a change that God is leading you in, I would love to hear about it. You can email me at hello@madetochangetheworld.com.

BEAUTIFUL MESS

If you are struggling with the things you are reading and wondering if this could be for you, here is something God showed me as I was flying over the Midwest section of the United States. I was listening to a song by Hillsong United titled "So Will I (100 billion X)". The lyrics talk about God's creation and the power of His voice to create all that we see, and the thought came to me that it is a "beautiful mess".

As I look at the masterpiece of this earth that God created outside my plane window, I realize that it is also a mess because we made it that way. From the first sin in the Garden of Eden, the wrong choices we (humans) have made have led to hate, death, worry, fear, and all the other bad things you can think of in this world. Yet, I see God's very creation yearning to be back in right standing with its Creator.

His greatest creation, however, is not what I see outside the plane but what I see in it. God's most exceptional day and his finest hour were when He made us in His image. Even though we have become a mess ourselves, God desires, above all else, to be close to us and calls to us, just like Jesus did to Peter, to be with Him to change the world.

You may not feel worthy. You may feel a mess from your past, yet you are beautiful to God. Do not be a captive to your mess; turn it all over Jesus. Do not hold anything back. It does not matter where you were born, what you have or do not have, what you have done, or what has been done to you. It doesn't matter your race, your age, or your gender. The One who created you loves you and calls out to you. **Your life matters. You were made to change the world.**

2 Chronicles 7:14 (NIV) says, "If my people, who are called by my name, will humble themselves and pray and seek my face and turn from their wicked ways, then I will hear from heaven, and I will forgive their sin and will heal their land."

You are one of God's children. He calls you by name. Humble yourself before God and seek Him. This is the very first step you must take in self-control. God will not force you to come to Him, but He will bless you and use you when you do. When you do this, He will take away your mess. If all His children did the same thing, He would take away the mess of the entire world.

As I listened through the song another time, some lyrics stuck out to me, which are: "If creation still obeys you, so will I. If the stars were made to worship, so will I. If everything exists to lift you high, so will I."

Bible Verse:

Proverbs 16:3 (NIV) – "Commit to the Lord whatever you do, and He will establish your plans."

Prayer:

Dear Jesus, thank you for your plan for me. I believe you have plans to prosper me and not harm me. Plans to give me hope and a future. I seek you with all my heart. Show me the things you have for me and want me to change, pursue, or create. I love you and trust you, Lord. Lead me to love others and do your will. In Jesus' Name, Amen.

Take Action:

1. Ask God what He wants you to change or pursue over the next several months.
2. Decide if you will commit to His calling. If you do, then make a plan and get support.

Additional Resources:

Book - *Over the Top* and *The Performance Planner* by Zig Ziglar

Movie – *Chariots of Fire* Produced by David Puttnam

Music – "Trust in You" by Lauren Daigle

Tool - *Theology of Behavior Change* - www.madetochangetheworld.com/resources

CHAPTER 6
ROLLING THROUGH LIFE

C hapter Focus: *So far in this book, we have covered the important areas of purpose, truth, and faith. Hopefully, you are excited about the future. Now it is time to take those concepts into the practical world of real life. Having the desire to live a life of purpose that is based on truth and faith is extremely important. How does this translate into the daily life you live and the challenges of this world? This chapter will help you see the main areas of your life in light of how God desires them to be. You will know what is working and determine areas where God leads you to focus. As you will learn, awareness is the first step to change. This chapter will show you more about yourself and where God wants to lead you.*

LIGHTS, CAMERA, ACTION

My sister Amy worked in Hollywood for many years at one of the big studios. I had several opportunities to see the filming of various shows, one of which was *Frazier* starring Kelsey Grammer. In this particular episode, Kelsey's back went out and he was struggling for most of the show.

When the director said, "Lights, camera, action," Kelsey became a man crippled with pain, bent over and barely able to walk. It was one of the best performances I had ever seen. When the director said, "cut," he walked perfectly normally, was free from pain, and there were absolutely no back issues. He could snap into and out of character in an instant. It was as if he were two different people. As far as an acting career, this is impressive work. However, in real-life, acting like two different people is destructive.

I recently heard a statistic that less than 10% of those who attend church or say they are Christians actually live what they claim. Like Kelsey in his show, most believers live two different lives. There is the life we act out at church, at Bible study, or in a small group, and then there is the life we live the rest of the time. Anyone can put on a show and act the part for a few hours a week. It takes real courage and self-control to live the life to which God calls us when we are outside the church walls.

Your life's "Lights, camera, action" does not start when you pull into a church parking lot, and the "cut" doesn't occur when we drive home. The real "Lights, camera, action" started when you left your mother's womb and entered this world. What you live each day is real life. Your growth, decisions, and purpose don't just happen part of the time. We don't take a break from living until the final day we are on this earth, which is when we hear "cut" and leave this scene.

This life is not a show. Instead, it is a reality, and the director (of the world) knows the "scene" you are in every moment of every day. He knows the purpose and plan for that "scene" of your life. The script for your life is written to be a fantastic story of love, victory, fulfillment, and impact. Now you have to live it.

ROLLING THROUGH LIFE

Imagine that the way to roll through life is like riding a bicycle. Bicycles are fantastic and fun. They can take you to many places and can give you experiences you can't get in a car or even walking. You can ride your bike along the road and go very quickly to your destination. You can ride near the beach and enjoy the scenery. You can ride in the mountains and get an adrenaline rush by managing all the twists and turns. Life is really like riding a bike through all the places and areas where God leads you.

There are some essential parts of this "bike of life". Arguably, the brakes are the most important, because even if you can't pedal well, once you start rolling downhill, you really do need your brakes. You may say that the next most important thing on the bike is the seat. If you have ridden bikes before, you may actually put this as number one.

I am going to suggest the most important parts, along with brakes, are the wheels and tires. Without those being round, in place, and solid, you really wouldn't go anywhere. Imagine a bike with a bent wheel and broken spokes. You would not only have a bumpy ride but it would be tough to get anywhere at all. The wheels need to be round, durable, and the right size. Even if you have strong, round wheels they may be too small. In that case, you are going to be pedaling extremely hard to get anywhere in life.

Imagine that your life bike has all the best parts. You have fantastic brakes and your seat is as comfy as a La Z Boy chair (let me know when you find one of those). Let's also imagine that your wheels are large with strong spokes. The tires are inflated and in place. Your chain is sturdy and oiled. Now you are ready for a fantastic ride. Don't forget your helmet.

Here's how these bike parts compare to your life:

The brakes – Self-control (based on what was talked about in the last chapter)

The seat – Living your purpose each day

The wheels and tires – Your balance in life that will be covered next

The oiled chain – Your daily walk with God (praying and reading the Bible)

The helmet – Knowing the truth for your life.

Earlier in the book, we covered the importance of knowing and living by the truth. We also spent significant time discussing self-control. The importance of daily time with God was also reviewed. The next two areas are your life balance and perseverance in following your path.

THE MYSTERY OF BALANCE

There is so much discussion about life balance or work/life balance and the importance of having it in place. The problem is trying to define what life balance is. Let's first start by describing what it is not. Being out of balance means that someone or something, other than God, is taking up more of your time, energy, and resources than it should. Being out of balance ultimately means that God is not first and that He is not the direction you follow in all areas of your life.

Being out of balance, or better defined as not having God at your center, feels like stress, worry, doubt, fatigue, burnout, never being caught up, or never being good enough. Out of balance means out of peace. Philippians 4:7 says, "The peace of God, which surpasses all understanding, will guard your hearts and minds through Christ Jesus." When God is at the center of all areas of your life, you have peace in knowing that He will take care of things out of your control.

Being out of balance means that you are trying to do everything your-self. It means you are taking on all the tasks, all the pressure, and all the responsibility in life. Being in balance means being in Christ and knowing that you are doing the best you can in all areas of life that you manage.

One definition of balance is, "keep or put something in a steady posi-tion so that it does not fall." That is precisely what God does for us when we fully trust and follow Him in every situation and area of life. When we try to control things with our own wisdom, strength, and energy we are not only out of balance, but we are headed for failure. It is important to remember that you are not God.

The world's definition of balance is that everything in life should be operating at peak performance based on the world's definition of success. You will never achieve this. It is impossible! The world's definition and God's definition are two different things. Let's look at the life of the most balanced person who ever walked the face of the earth: Jesus.

Jesus was Himself perfect in every way because He is God. This means He is also our model for life balance. By the world's standards, He was out of balance in most areas of His life.

When you look at Jesus' "career", he quit his responsible job as a carpenter at age thirty. He then became what would be considered a mix between a prophet, religious leader, and priest. In those days the responsible way to have that job would be to take a formal position with regular hours at the temple. Jesus did none of this. He didn't have an official "job" and he didn't have a stable home. Jesus was a wanderer, going from town to town and house to house preaching good news and healing the sick. By today's standards, he would have been a failure in both his job and managing a household. Jesus also didn't have a solid financial plan based on today's standards. He simply had faith to believe that as he did the Father's will, his Dad would provide in every way. There were no 401ks, stock options or even savings accounts. Don't get me wrong--none of these are bad things. The key is that Jesus' priority was not things. His priority was knowing and following His Father, and believing God would take care of Him. So far, Jesus doesn't seem very balanced.

Let's look at his relationships next. In one way, what Jesus did was fantastic. He traveled with 12 guys and they were all very close. However, Jesus never really settled down to have continual close friends and a family. He even ticked off some of His close friends and at one point called one of them Satan. I am not sure how that tactic would fit in with Dale Carnegie's book *How to Win Friends and Influence People,* but I am guessing it is not near the top of the list. The other problem Jesus had with others is that he was hated by many religious leaders because he was disrupting their world.

You can look at other areas such as health, time management, recreation, etc. and Jesus would miss the mark according to the way the world measures success and balance. So how should life balance be measured? It is having all areas of your life led by God and living them as best you can. To gauge how you are doing, ask God if you are living according to His Word in each area of your life. Are you letting God be the lead and bless you, or are you taking the lead and hoping God will bless what you decide?

The truth of the matter is that balance is a misconception. You cannot, and will not, have every area in your life operating at 100% the way you would like, because all the variables around us continuously change. For example, if you were to rank 1-10 how you feel you are doing in your career, you may base your ranking on what you think your title should be, how much responsibility you should have, or the amount of money you feel you should be making. The truth of the matter is that you don't control these things. The better questions for real balance in this area of life are:

Am I working where God wants me to be working right now?

Am I working at what God calls me to do with all my heart?

Am I trusting in God for my provision vs. trusting in myself?

Would God say "well done" regarding what I did today?

The judge of how you are doing in life is not the world or even yourself; it is God. This goes directly back to spending time each day with God, reading His Word, talking with Him through prayer, then following as He leads. This is why Jesus was perfectly balanced in life. He went off by himself to pray in the early morning or after a big day. Many times, he would get near water or walk in nature. Jesus always knew exactly what God the Father wanted him to do and he did it.

The first and most important area to evaluate is your spiritual life. Are you spending time with God to get His direction, peace, and power through the Holy Spirit? Do you know and follow God's plan for all areas of your life? In the next section, there is a picture of "balance" that will help you clearly see how you are doing.

. . .

Ultimately, when you have balance in your life, you are continuing to let God "put you in a steady position so that you will not fall" by putting Him first and living His way. When you are in balance, you are at peace. This does not mean everything is going perfectly in life. What it does mean is that you are surrendered to God, living for Him as best you can and trusting in His results.

THE SURRENDER WHEEL

In coaching, we use what is called a Balance Wheel or Coaching Mandala. Essentially, this wheel helps a person take stock of all the areas of his/her life to see where things are working well and where attention is needed. It is a powerful tool to build awareness. I use it at the beginning of each coaching session to help clients see their life more clearly and determine overall well-being.

The wheel is powerful, because awareness is the first key to change. If you aren't aware of something, you don't know it needs to be altered. I took the balance wheel idea a step further to build more awareness about our walk with God. A good friend of mine, Erik Landvick (author of *Uncluttered Faith*), noticed the wheel should show how well we are surrendered to God versus how we are controlling our own lives. From that idea I created a Christian Surrender Wheel. It is based on scripture and helps show how surrendered you are to God. It is one thing to say you surrender your life to God, and quite another to do it. You cannot fulfill your purpose if you are not living for God in all areas of life.

This new tool helps you look more closely at the areas of life where God wants you to glorify Him. It is a starting point. It will help you see where you are living based on God's desires and other areas that need to be changed. Ultimately, if you are living any part of life based on your own opinions or desires, it is not what He has planned for you and will impact all other areas of your life. The Christian Surrender Wheel is a tool and not a "be all, end all" solution. It provides a starting point to take stock of where you currently are in life, where God desires you to be, and what you need to surrender. The Wheel is an assessment God can use to help you realize new areas of growth.

The true gauge to measure and manage your life will always be God's Word and the Holy Spirit.

Before we look at each area of the wheel, it is important to note that neglecting any one area of life can cripple the others. For instance, if you glorify God in all areas except finances, you will always be under stress about money. The financial struggle would then impact your mental health, physical health, relationships, etc. This is the case for any area of life, since every area should glorify God.

For example, going back to finances, having a high number in that area does not mean you are one of the top 100 billionaires in the world. It is just the opposite. It merely means that in the way you live your life, no matter how much or how little you have, you are using it in the way God desires you to use it.

Keep in mind that there is no "perfect" level you can achieve in these areas of life. Perfection in this world was gone right after the first sin and our removal from the Garden of Eden. What we are to strive for is holiness and righteousness. Holiness means being set apart by God because of our relationship with Him, and Righteousness means being in right standing with God because of how we submit to him in our daily lives.

The goal is not to have all 10's on your Surrender Wheel. That is neither realistic nor practical. It is realistic to have 7-9 most of the time and in most areas. Life happens, we get caught off guard, things come up, and we have to adjust, so we are learning each day and won't be perfect. However, a generally larger bike wheel, as described in the *Rolling Through Life* section, will provide a much better ride over life's bumps.

A word to the wise: This Wheel is not to condemn you, but instead to encourage you. This is the start of where God can show you His plan and next steps through His power. It is the first place to understand where you are and where God wants you to be. In the next chapter I will help you learn ways to make the changes toward which God is calling you.

Here are the areas that make up the Christian Surrender Wheel:

1) **Spiritual:** Mark 12:30 (NIV) "Love the Lord your God with all your heart and with all your soul and with all your mind and with all your strength."

2) **Mental:** Proverbs 29:18 (NIV) "Where there is no vision, the people perish."

3) **Physical:** 1 Cor 3:16-19 (NIV) "Don't you know that you yourselves are God's temple and that God's Spirit lives in you? If anyone destroys God's temple, God will destroy him; for God's temple is sacred, and you are that temple."

4) **Family:** Proverbs 11:29 (NIV) "He who brings trouble on his family will only inherit the wind."

5) **Relationships:** Mark 12:31 (NIV) "The second (commandment) is this: 'Love your neighbor as you love yourself.' There is no commandment greater than these."

6) **Career:** Colossians 3:23 (NIV) "Whatever you do, work at it with all your heart as working for the Lord, not for man, since you know that you will receive an inheritance from the Lord as a reward. It is the Lord Christ you are serving."

7) **Finances:** Hebrews 13:5 (NIV) "Keep your lives free from the love of money and be content with what you have."

8) **Recreation:** Deuteronomy 16:14 (NIV) "Be joyful at your Feast—you, your sons and daughters..."

THE OUTER CIRCLE OF THE WHEEL, OR THE RIM, IS MADE UP OF THREE additional areas:

1) **Attitude:** Philippians 2:5 (NIV) "Your attitude should be the same as that of Christ Jesus."

2) **Time:** Proverbs 20:4 (NIV) "A sluggard does not plow in season, so at harvest time he looks but finds nothing."

3) **Talents:** 1 Peter 4:10 (NIV) "Each of you should use whatever gift you have received to serve others, as faithful stewards of God's grace in its various forms."

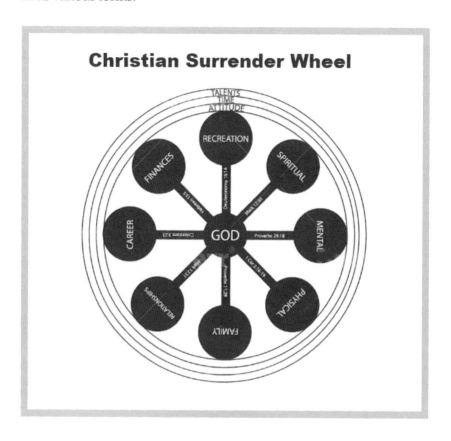

Take the assessment by ranking 1-10 how surrendered to God you are in each area:

1) **Spiritual:**

2) **Mental:**

3) **Physical**:

4) **Family:**

5) **Relationships:**

6) **Career:**

7) **Finances:**

8) **Recreation:**

TOTAL SCORE:

Take a look at your total score. If it is over 65, that means you have a good overall balance. If it is under 65, you can probably feel your life out of balance with God. What area is the highest? You can probably think of reasons why that is so high. What area is the lowest? You can probably also think of reasons why it is so low. In the next chapter, we will cover how to make changes in the area of life you feel God calling you to work on.

How are you doing with the outer circle of the rim?

1) **Attitude:**

2) **Time:**

3) **Talents:**

TOTAL SCORE

If your score is under a 25, you probably have some things you would like to improve because these areas directly relate to you fulfilling your purpose in life. Ask yourself the same questions listed above for the other eight areas of the balance wheel, such as what areas are the highest and lowest and what you feel God would have you work on.

Use this tool. Print it out and evaluate yourself at least once per week. Pray for God's wisdom and direction on how to use what you learn. Partner for support with a coach, mentor, or accountability partner. Here is the link to take this assessment online www. madetochangetheworld.com / assessment. Some additional wheels and assessments delve deeper into each area. If you wish to delve deeper into this area for your life, you can read another book written by Kathy Swigle and myself titled *Life Balance for Christians: It's Not What You Think*. These resources can also be found on the website listed above.

Once you take the assessment, plot your answers on the wheel, then connect the dots. You will most likely notice you don't have a good, smooth, and perfect wheel. Going back to the example we had earlier in this chapter, this is currently the wheel you have on your "bike of life". How smooth is your ride? Would you put that on your actual bike today and try to ride on it? Perhaps it is a jagged wheel and not a very easy ride.

An important note is that you could have a very balanced wheel by having all low numbers, such as 3's, 2's or 1's in your life. The good news is that it rolls. The bad news is that it is so small. It has to turn twice as fast as a normal-sized wheel does to get anywhere. It is too small for your life. Small wheels will quickly burn you out because nothing is working as God designed. You will be pedaling that "bike of life" so hard that you burn out from exhaustion and then fall over. Work on enlarging your wheel, and as you surrender, your ride will become much smoother.

As I stated earlier, this Wheel is not intended to condemn you but to encourage you. This starting point is where God can show you His plan and His next steps. It is the first place to understand where you are and where God wants you to be. This awareness is something to pray about and ask for God's direction. The next chapter will cover how to change these areas of life. The foundation and confidence for any Godly changes will come from your relationship with Him.

Have fun using this tool. Don't put too much pressure on yourself. The only perfect person was Jesus. We are in right standing with God because of what Jesus did for us and not our works. Realize that these things make up your life and are supported by your faith, hope, and love for God. Your ultimate goal is to hear Jesus and live by following Him. He will give you the power to do so through the Holy Spirit.

Not having your wheel where you desire is a beautiful thing because God will use it to bring a greater closeness with Him. This is not about performance. It is about relationship. Be gracious and kind to yourself as you draw close to the Father who loves you and will be with you to show you the way. He will help you use what He gave you.

One additional insight from my friend Erik Landvik is that he considers our greatest calling to be disciples of Jesus. The word disciple means "disciplined one". God asks us to discipline ourselves. He helps us follow Him in order to receive His promises. Don't fear the unknown. Don't fear failure. Don't fear success. Fear is not from God. Love and obey him, then watch what He will do in your life. God has a great plan for you. There is nothing to fear by following Him.

THE HUB

The Surrender Wheel is a symbol of the parts of life. The most important thing to understand is what is at the hub of that wheel where it connects to the axle. A wheel is only as strong as what it is placed upon. For example, if the wheel we have been talking about was a stagecoach wheel, it would carry much weight and many people. The wheel would be useless if it was not placed on a solid iron or steel axle. If that axle was not strong, the wheel would easily bend or break, causing injury.

The hub for our wheel of life must be God if we are to have any chance of purpose, fulfillment, and impact in this life. Your hub for your life must be based on the truth and power of God to get the blessing and promises of God in every area of your life. Thankfully, God gives us timeless direction in each of these areas and shows us how to live to place our lives on the ultimate hub: God.

Although the wheel we have been talking about is not literal, it is something visual that can be applied to all areas of life. If you find an area you need to work on, likely starting with your weakest spoke, there is a separate wheel for that. For instance, "career" is made up of multiple spokes to strengthen that particular area. It shows you how God wants you to live that aspect of your life and what to work on. You can find the additional wheels in the book mentioned above called *Life Balance for Christians: It's Not What You Think* found at www. madetochangetheworld.com.

Once God becomes the axle--the very center of every area of your life-- and permeates every spoke, He is the power driving the shaft and moving your "wheel of life" that powers your life to move forward.

THE RUT

Here is a funny story related to stagecoach wheels to show the power of how we live. Many years ago when early settlers were migrating across the United States to the West, they did so in stagecoaches and covered wagons. Over time, they started to form trails and paths that other adventurers could follow. Since the wheels on the stagecoaches were big and skinny, they began to build roads that were just ruts that got deeper and deeper.

These tracks got so deep at specific points that once a wheel was in them it became difficult to get out. At a spot in Colorado, there was a fork in the road and each stagecoach driver had to determine which way to go – left or right. At the decision point where each driver had to make a critical choice, there was a sign that read, "choose your rut wisely; you are going to be in it a long time."

When it comes to the tracks we follow in life, our brains develop similar ruts. Whatever you choose to do over and over forms mental ruts and habits that become tough to change. But they can be changed, and over time you can develop new "ruts" that keep your life going in the direction God desires.

The moral of the story is to not only have a strong and balanced wheel for your life by having God at the very hub, but to make sure you are running the wheel on the right track. The road is what will determine your destination. The habits you form from thinking and doing certain things over and over will get you to your destination, which will either be one God desires for you or an endpoint that is off-course. Therefore, "Choose your rut wisely; you're going to be in it a long time."

As you are probably realizing, reading about all of this is one thing, but doing something about it is quite another. There is a great quote that you may already know. Years ago, someone coined the term "Knowledge is power." Later, someone expanded upon this quote to say "Applied knowledge is power." I will take that even a step further to say, "Applied knowledge and wisdom from God are His power in you." The next chapter is all about how to make changes in life that God is calling you to make.

Bible Verse:

Colossians 3:17 (ESV) – "And whatever you do, in word or deed, do everything in the name of the Lord Jesus, giving thanks to God the Father through him."

Prayer:

Lord Jesus, life can be so hard, as you already said it would be. But you also promised that you would never leave me or forsake me and that I can do all things through you who strengthen me. Help me to live all areas of my life to honor you. Amen.

Take Action:

1. Take the assessment from earlier in this chapter.
2. Pray about the first area God would have you work on to reflect more on His purpose.

Additional Resources:

Book - *Christian Surrender Wheel* by Brian Williams and Kathy Swigle (Spring 2020)

Movie – *I Can Only Imagine* Produced by Kevin Downes Productions / Mission Pictures

Music – "I Can Only Imagine" by Mercy Me

Tool - *Christian Surrender Wheel* www.madetochangetheworld.com / resources

CHAPTER 7
MOVE FORWARD

C hapter Focus: *Most people have things they want to change or do in life and can't get themselves to take action. Maybe you can relate. This chapter of the book is about moving forward. It is one thing to say you are going to do something and quite another thing to do it. Many obstacles can hold you back from taking action in this world, including fear and not knowing what to do next. This chapter will address not only what may be standing in your way, but also the importance of taking action. It will also help you break through what may be holding you back in the most important areas of your life. Now that you have new awareness from writing your Purpose, Mission, and Vision Statements and checking your Life Balance, we will cover how to make the right decisions, follow God's plan, and then faithfully execute it.*

SURPRISE

You are going to be so thrilled! I have a big (hypothetical) surprise for you. I built you a new home! It's a beautiful 4,000-square-foot house with a lake behind it, near the mountains and completely paid for. I made sure you have a cleaning lady, a maid, and a butler to go with it. It is stocked with food and everything you need.

It is already complete and waiting for you; all you have to do is come and live in it. It is in a beautiful area and you can bring whomever you want to live with you. The town is full of friendly, supportive, and loving people. There are many fun things to do, and I know you will be fulfilled there. You will love it! I guarantee it.

However, I am not going to force you to go. Although the place is finished and ready, you have to choose to go there. You must believe me enough to claim it for yourself. I even bought you your favorite car to get there. You know, the one you always thought that "one day if I ever have the money, I am going to buy it." I even got it in your favorite color. I made your accommodations for the long drive there and made sure you have a fantastic GPS.

Now, it's your turn. You have to decide if you believe me. If you do trust me, then you will need to pack your new car, get in it with your loved ones and drive. On your way there, you are going to need to follow the GPS carefully. You are also going to need to obey all the traffic signs and speed limits along the way.

I am sure you are excited! If you could, you might want to drive 100 miles an hour and blow through all the red lights to make it sooner. However, if you don't drive carefully, you could get into an accident, be pulled over, miss your GPS route, or even run out of gas. No matter how great the house is, how well the car runs, and how accurate the GPS navigation, you are the one who is responsible for driving safely by obeying the traffic laws, sticking to the speed limit, and following the route to get there.

You choose if you will claim the new house or not. You elect to follow the rules or not. You decide if you will listen to the GPS or try to find your own way. You decide if you are going to go all the way or go part way and settle for a town in between. You can even stay living exactly as you are now even though everything I promised you--and more--is waiting. The choice is up to you and you alone.

Unfortunately, I do not have the car or the house for you, so don't pack your bags quite yet. However, this analogy is based on the plan God has for you in this life on earth. If you have accepted Jesus in your heart, then one day you will go to be with Him in heaven and live in your eternal home. But don't miss what God has for you here. There is an amazing journey He has planned for you. While this life is not all blue skies and roses, He does promise you will have complete peace, unshakable joy, deep fulfillment, and great love as you follow Him. Will it lead to beautiful cars and new homes? Only God knows, but those aren't the most important things in this life. The most important things are not things. What is most important is to know you are with Him on the path He has for you every day. There is no greater fulfillment at the end of each day than to hear God say to you, "Well done, good and faithful servant." That is the purpose worth living for.

How can you live in a way that keeps you along His path, doing the right things and knowing in your heart you would hear "well done" from God? The answer is in knowing Him, knowing His Word, then doing what He calls you to do.

COMMIT TO ACT

Commitment is probably the most powerful principle there is for your spiritual life. God has been committed to you since day one! He said He would never leave or forsake you. If that is not a commitment, I do not know what is. He commits that when you believe His son Jesus died for you and you accept him as Lord of your life, you become His child and are saved. He even sends His Holy Spirit to live inside you to lead and guide your steps.

Commitment at the spiritual level is directly tied to faith. If you have committed yourself to God, you have committed to knowing His will and vision for your life and to living that out every day. This is the core of Christian living! If all of your commitments are in line with God's plan for you, you can be assured that no matter what happens, your commitment to walking by faith will lead you to greater things than you can ever ask or imagine.

Commitment is the link that ties thinking about something into taking action. A commitment turns your decision into a plan. In addition to the definitions of commitment in Chapter 5, here are a couple of additional ones from *Merriam-Webster**:

1: the trait of sincere and steadfast fixity of purpose;

2: the act of binding yourself (intellectually or emotionally) to a course of action

The first definition does not beat around the bush. It tells it like it is. Commitment is the absolute focus of mind, emotion, will, and physical ability toward a goal or purpose until it is accomplished. The only time that commitment changes is if it is impossible to continue pursuing, or internal beliefs change (such as God-given redirection).

The second means that when you commit to something completely, you are now a part of it and it is a part of you. It is so deep that it becomes part of your intellect, emotional makeup, and mindset. If you have ever had the experience of using Super Glue and accidentally gluing your fingers to each other or something else – they become one. You have to rip the object, or worse, the skin, to get them apart. Commitment is like super glue and not like the glue substance on the back of Post It Notes that holds papers together only minimally and pulls apart with any amount of pressure exerted.

Commitment is more than just words. It is action or inaction (such as not pursuing another relationship to stay faithful to your spouse). Although the word commitment is a noun, its very definition includes the activity of fulfilling the commitment that was made. If an obligation is completed, it is a fulfilled promise.

When you commit to someone or something, you bind to it and become one with it. You will know you have made a commitment when you have only one possible outcome – fulfilling it. When you give your word to someone and commit to it, the way you follow through on that commitment becomes a reflection of who you are. You will quickly gain confidence in yourself when you fulfill something you have committed to complete. You will lose confidence in yourself when you commit to something and do not complete it, even if no one but you knows about it.

Before committing to something, especially a big commitment (such as marriage, buying a house, starting a business, etc.), it is essential to know what you are committing to and why you are committing to it. Realize that you may have to sacrifice a lot (maybe everything) to fulfill it. If this decision is in line with what God is calling you to do, He will help you achieve it.

There are many different things you can commit to in life. You can commit to something as simple as reading a book or something as challenging as moving to another country. Important to note is that the result of your commitment may end up different from what you initially intended because there may be many things out of your control. If you commit to the things God wants you to, He is in charge of the outcome.

In a wedding ceremony, the bride and groom make a commitment to each other before God and man. These commitments do not get fulfilled that day; they get fulfilled over a lifetime. It is quite easy to say that you will stick with someone "for better or worse, for richer or poorer, in sickness and in health" while you are standing in front of everyone excited and full of joy for the occasion. It is quite different several years down the road to remember and stick to that commitment when finances are tight, struggles are pressing, and one (or both) of you is feeling sick and tired. That is where the test of commitment takes place--not because of the words once said, but because of the actions taken in the middle of the trials.

Just because you made a commitment and are keeping that commitment, it does not guarantee success, at least perhaps not in the way you imagine it will happen. You may have committed to start a business and it didn't work out. You may have given it your best and kept your commitment to the end. If you followed God's will in doing this, there might have been a bigger purpose in it than you may have seen. In all the commitments you make, He will help you keep them. In the times where things do not go as you planned, Romans 8:28 says that "God works all things together for good for those who love Him and are called according to His purpose." Don't lose faith. Don't give up. Give God time to work.

Be careful when changing or abandoning any commitment, because human nature is to make excuses or give up in the face of adversity. Ask yourself some questions if you are considering changing or quitting a commitment:

1. Have I kept my commitment so far?
2. Why do I feel I need to change or quit this commitment?
3. Is there anything I can do to help this move forward?
4. Am I giving up because of worry, fear, or feeling stuck?
5. Are these circumstances entirely out of my control?
6. What are the possible solutions to make this work?
7. What is God telling me to do? (most important)

YOU MAY WONDER HOW TO ANSWER THE FINAL QUESTION AND KNOW WHAT God wants you to do. This requires several things to come into agreement. The first is God's Word and what you are finding in the Bible. The second is what you are sensing through prayer; as you seek God, over time you will sense peace in the right direction and decision. The third is looking to see what God is showing you through other circumstances, such as closed doors or things just starting to fit together as you seek Him.

FLY BY PLANS

In the amazing time when we now live, the size of the world seems small. We can cover a distance of 2,500 miles in just a few short hours. If you live in New York and need to get to Los Angeles, you can get there very quickly. I had a coaching client one time who flew on a jet called the Concord, and his flight enabled him to have breakfast in Europe, New York, and Los Angeles all on the same day. Can you imagine watching the sunrise for the same day three times in a row? What once took months now takes minutes.

Today's jets allow you to cover a lot of ground in a short time. However, that is not what is most important! For example, imagine you are leaving Chicago in hopes of being in Tampa for your best friend's wedding the next day. Imagine you are flying at 30,000 feet and going 500 MPH but now seeing the Rocky Mountains and the Pacific Ocean. When you finally land at a private airport near Baja, Mexico because you were running out of fuel, you wonder what happened.

You later find out that the pilot of your plane likes to fly wherever and whenever, without any real agenda, through the "wild blue yonder." This time his course took the flight, and you, on an adventure outside the U.S. Because he did not have a specific target, or goal, it messed up the plans for you and all the other passengers. Although this is an exaggeration, it does reflect the importance of having direction and a plan while traveling fast through life. Otherwise, you may find yourself in the middle of nowhere lost and "running out of gas."

You may look at this plane story and think that it is irresponsible not to consider where you are going and completely miss your destination. You may also read it and think how fun it would be just to fly where the wind takes you. In life, you will generally find people who default more to one of these given motives. People usually consider themselves to be either structured or unstructured. Other terms that may be used are creative vs. logical or artsy compared to organized.

Whichever you consider yourself to lean toward, there is good news. God created us to be both and have balance. We are made in God's image. Therefore, when you look at who God is and what He made, He is very creative. Everything you see, He made. When you watch a sunset or see water ripples, it is the most fabulous art ever created. He also is organized and structured. Every day the sun rises and sets. Every year we go through four seasons. Our very lives have a flow from baby, to child, to adult, to senior.

In other words, we are to have organization and structure in our lives as led by God to hear Him more, follow Him closely, and be creative in all the ways He made us so. Following God is a complete adventure. After you commit, then make a plan. Make commitments as led by God. Then make plans to act on your promise, also as directed by God. Then remember Proverbs 16:9: "In his heart, a man plans his course, but the Lord determines His steps." There is an old quote that says,

"People don't plan to fail; they fail to plan." Also remember: a commitment is not a commitment unless you act on it. The only way to be successful is to have a plan that will get you going. Then let God adjust it as He desires, as you live the adventure with Him.

GOOD VS. BAD COMMITMENTS

You make decisions daily, hourly, and sometimes minute by minute. Those decisions are what will determine your future and how closely you walk with God because decisions lead to commitments and action

We all make bad decisions at times. This can be due to many reasons, including our selfishness, not hearing God or even seeking Him, getting very emotional or tired, and the list goes on. Some bad decisions have small effects, like eating a Stromboli right before bed, then having heartburn all night. Other bad choices can have severe impacts, such as deciding to drive drunk. God allows us to make all of our own decisions, but will show us how to be wise if we let Him. As a side note, Proverbs is a book in the Bible that is entirely about living by wisdom. Billy Graham had a great suggestion: Reading one of the 31 books of Proverbs each day of the month. One book of Proverbs struck me heavily about wisdom's impact on every area of life. I even wrote a book about it called *Win with God Today* (which can be found at www.madetochangetheworld.com).

When we do not have wisdom or seek God, or when we act on emotions, we can get ourselves into significant messes. God's chosen people, Israel, got themselves in a colossal mess many centuries ago and still pay for it to this day. The story, from Joshua 9, goes like this.

When Joshua was leading Israel to the promised land, they took down a couple of major cities of the day. One was Jericho and the other named Ai. When other people around them heard about this, they were terrified. One such group, called the Gibeonites, came up with a deceptive scheme and succeeded.

They sent a delegate to the leaders of Israel saying that they had come from a faraway land and wanted to have peace with Israel. The Gibeonites looked the part, sounded the part, and had a plausible story. When Joshua inquired as to who they were and where they came from, they made up a story and asked for a truce with Israel. Since everything they saw and heard seemed to check out, Israel signed an agreement with them. The most important thing they missed was to pray and ask God for wisdom. God would have shown Israel the truth, but instead, three days after the declaration signing, Israel found out that they had been deceived by the neighboring enemy and were contractually stuck in their agreement, which has haunted them ever since.

It is better to learn from history than to repeat the mistakes ourselves. There is an enemy named the Devil who continually looks for ways to wreck your life. Do not fear, though, because God is on your side and is much stronger than this enemy. Your principal responsibility in all of this is to seek God, hear God, and know God. He will lead you to make all the best and right decisions for your future. His wisdom will give you all He has planned for your life. Living by your own wisdom will get you into a mess.

THE PLAN

I love the Asian proverb I heard many years ago, which says, "The man who says, 'it cannot be done' should not interrupt the one doing it." The rest of this chapter will cover the crucial life aspect of turning thoughts into action, with specific focus on the importance of habits and overcoming fear. As a reminder, all of this is built on having faith in God and trusting Him to act upon whatever He calls you to think, say, or do. Simply having faith in yourself or anyone else will either freeze you in fear or take you down the wrong road.

Unfortunately, the place where you will find the biggest and most plentiful dreams is the cemetery. There are many things that could have been done, changed, and improved in this world, but people took their visions with them to the grave. They gave into fear or never put a plan into place to legitimately take action on what they believed in. Those dreams will never become a reality in their lives. God could have led them to find the cure for cancer, to start a revival, or to speak the words to bring their grandpa to Jesus. Don't let this be you. God has an important purpose for your life as discussed earlier in this book. God will not force you to move upon your plan. However, He will be there to guide, empower, and support you every step of the way when you choose to follow Him.

Plans are established through goals. Goals are strategies and commitments for how you will use your time, talent, and treasures. The importance of goals is that they enable you to move your God-given dream into action. If you have a vision for your future but no plan, you will not achieve it! Vision gives you hope for your future while goals allow you to plan on how to make that vision a reality. A quote that I keep in front of me is based on Proverbs 29:18: "Where there is no vision, the people perish." It says, "A vision without a task is a dream; A task without a vision is drudgery; A vision and a task is the hope of the world."

When setting goals for your future, always be sure that they are in line with God's calling based on His Word and direction. They should always line up with your Purpose, Mission, and Vision Statements (if they don't, you may need to change your statements). Sometimes, you will work on actions that are not exciting or even appearing to move you quickly ahead, but are important stepping-stones for your growth and future. You will know if a goal is right because you will have peace as you pray about it, although it may be a scary stretch for you. Just thinking about accomplishing it should give you energy and move you toward the vision God has given you.

You may sometimes feel that you are in a job or situation that has nothing to do with where God is ultimately leading you. Make sure to spend time with God to find out where He wants you. Do not rush on just because in your mind things do not fit. Sometimes it is time to move on, and He will show you how and when to do that. Sometimes He wants you to stay right where you are, and you may not know why, but make sure to remain faithful. He will show you His plan and lead you to set specific goals even though they may not make sense at the time to you.

Throughout my career, I have had many varied experiences in life including sales, leadership, ministry, etc. Two seemingly opposite careers were the first decade that I spent in the financial world, then the following two decades focused on behavior change. I felt like I had wasted my time in one or both of these careers and had not gotten anywhere. I will never forget a lunch I had with a good friend and mentor of mine, Seth Tuckerman, who is a brilliant businessman. He had just read a book about someone who went the first 40 years of his life with varied experiences that seemed completely disconnected, then all of a sudden they all came together in his new profession and he was propelled in growth. Seth believed that to be true of me as I was embarking on in my career--and he was right. I soon was leading a large staff of behavior change-focused coaches that drove our business, and I used my financial training to understand what that meant for outcomes and business success. I also found myself using all the other experiences I had been through in this new and exciting role.

Don't outpace God! Seek Him to find exactly where He wants you to be. Be faithful in being the best you can be in that very spot. Focus on growing and goals. Trust in God for your future. If the purpose and vision you have are really from Him, He will show you how to get there. Don't rush ahead and don't fall behind. Walk step by step and day by day in the ways He shows you, and even the smallest changes He calls you to make will have an impact.

SETTING GOALS

If you search for the word "goals" on the web, you will find page after page of results. You can find planners and processes. You will find people and organizations to support you in your goals. You can find classes, CDs, and videos about goal-setting. Our culture and generation are all about goals. Unfortunately, it has come to the point in this modern age where goals are set based upon what a person thinks or feels about life. In our culture, our achievement of goals defines who we are. I approach goals very differently and will show you how.

Let's start by defining the word goal, which is "the end toward which effort is directed" (Miriam Webster). The other definitions are sports-related, but one I will also quote here is "the terminal point of a race". I quote the second definition because Hebrews 12:1 says, "Therefore since we are surrounded by such a great cloud of witnesses, let us throw off everything that hinders and the sin that so easily entangles. And let us run with perseverance the race marked out for us."

Here is the process I will describe to set goals:

1. Dedicate time to spend with God
2. Spend some time reading God's Word
3. Pray and ask God to direct your heart and mind and give you wisdom
4. Review your Life Purpose, Mission, and Vision Statements (see Chapter 2)
5. Review your Life Balance Wheel
6. Ask God to reveal to you what He would like you to focus on now
7. Write down what He shows you

This is a powerful time with God. Every time I implement this process, which is usually twice per year, I have an excitement about how He is leading me. By doing this, you may end up with just one or two things or a whole big list that has been put on your mind. Either way, do not worry about having too many or too few focus areas; we will work that through. As a side note, there is a planner I have used for many years that I list below, as well as a couple of other things that can help you through this.

Now take a look at all the main areas God has shown you and pray for Him to show you what is most important to work on first. If you try to focus on more than one or two things at a time, you will get none of them done and will be frustrated. You may even scrap the whole process. Narrow your focus down to only one or two main areas you feel are most important and do not worry about the others. God will have time for those, and in some cases, you will be working on some of those while focusing on your priorities.

Now, we break down the big area into manageable parts. List all the "Action Items" (goals) you can think of that you need to accomplish for this vision to come to pass. For example, if you were going to get married, you would need to list ALL the things that you would need to do from now until the day of the wedding. We will cover prioritizing the list shortly. Someone once said that a goal well set is already mostly achieved. Although this may seem a little tedious to you, it takes mere minutes but can be life-changing. This is also why I highly recommend working with a coach or partnering with someone through this process.

NOW THAT IS FAITH

In a study done in 2006, it was estimated that about 3% of the population in the United States have written goals. It was also found that about 3% of that same US population were millionaires, most of whom have written goals. I am not trying to make everyone millionaires. However, success ties directly into planning for it. This does not mean that because you plan for success you will automatically have it, but it is pretty certain that if you do not plan for it, you will not.

When you are setting your goals, it is best to use F.A.I.T.H, as mentioned in Chapter five. This acronym will help you set the correct goals and enable you to focus on success versus being vague and frustrated:

F - Focused (specific) – You must have a clear, not vague, goal

A - Attainable (achievable) – You must believe it in faith or don't set it

I - Individual (for you) – Only set a goal for you, not someone else

T - Trackable (measurable) – Be able to track and prove you did it

H - Heartfelt (passionate) – You must be passionate, or it won't happen

When you make it a habit of approaching your goals this way, you will find you are highly motivated to achieve them and positioned to move forward because they are clear and will help you stay focused on your vision. Think smart and act accordingly. Also, study those who do succeed and follow suit.

Here is an example of a FAITH goal that will help you become successful:

"I will begin spending 10 minutes with God every day at 7:00 am by reading a chapter of the Bible and praying, and I will start tomorrow morning."

Here is an example of a NON-FAITH goal that will not succeed:

"I will start spending more time with God."

Write your two priority goals you came up with here:

Goal A -

Goal B -

Now, use this chart below and answer yes or no to each question. If you cannot answer "yes" for each item, your goals need to be adjusted or removed. Use this process for each goal you set and remember to only work on one or two at a time.

Goal A

Goal B

Is this goal Focused (specific)?

Is the goal Attainable?

Is the goal Individualized (for you)?

Is the goal Trackable?

Is it Heartfelt?

Were all the answers "yes"?

Review these goals daily and manage your time to accomplish them. A valuable lesson I have learned and still use to this day is to track my time. You will be surprised to find out why you are not accomplishing the things as you would like in life once you begin accounting for your time. If you even try it for one day, you will begin to change your habits of how you pursue your FAITH goals and use your time.

You may also be wondering about all the other goals you listed out and are not yet addressing at this time. Keep that list handy and as you move forward and accomplish a goal, look again at your list, pray to God about what is next, and plan out the same goal process.

The other key factor in being successful is accountability. How many goals have you set and let slip by without ever achieving them? Who knew about it? My guess is that you didn't have a success partner (coach, mentor, accountability partner, etc.) at the time. It is easy to let yourself miss a commitment, then another commitment, then finally forget about the whole thing when no one else is looking. Accountability is key! To get help with this, go to www. madetochangetheworld.com. Additionally, if you would like to become a Change the World Coach, you can also go to that website for more information.

One last point: Once you set your goal, ask yourself on a score of 1-10 how confident you are that you can achieve it. If you cannot give it at least an 8, you need to go back to the drawing board and adjust it so that you are highly confident you can get it done. It is better to set an easy goal to achieve success and build momentum than to set a hard goal and miss it. Achieving a goal, no matter how small it is, builds confidence. Missing a goal because it is unrealistic at that time will tear down your confidence. One of the best habits you can form is keeping your commitments to God, yourself, and others. Be wise and pray as you set your goals. God is with you.

RUN FOR THE GOAL TO WIN THE PRIZE

In the mid-1900s, a young boy in England had a goal to one day attend a top University to become a doctor. However, his family was middle class and had no money to save for this schooling. He did not let that hold him back! He was committed to his goal and began to use an ability he already had--running fast--in hopes that it could one day help him reach his goal. Every day he ran to and from school, which did not make him popular with the other boys who were much too lazy to do the same.

His running paid off. As his running became flawless, he stood out as a high school runner and was offered a scholarship at Oxford University. His running continued to improve, and he was offered the chance to run in the 1948 Olympics, but he chose instead to concentrate on his studies. In 1952, after his abilities had been highly publicized, he entered the Olympic Games. Unfortunately, the scheduling of the events provided little time to rest and in the final race, he took fourth place. The media criticized his result, blaming it on his unconventional training.

This media attention prompted Roger to set another goal--the biggest one of his life--to break the world record for the mile run. Even though he was a full-time medical student at that point, he believed he could reach this goal. Roger could only set aside 45 minutes per day to run. He kept setting and achieving incremental goals. By 1954 he was ready for the challenge. On May 6th, Roger ran in a race with a couple of friends, whom he asked to set an incredible pace by running the first laps in 3 minutes; he was then on his own for the fourth. He crossed the finish line that day doing what no other human on record in history had done – he broke the 4-minute mile. Modern science had already "proven" that a human could not run that fast until Roger Bannister did.

What is the goal that you need to set and work toward that could change your life?

OVERCOMING FEAR

I cannot address setting goals, making commitments, and taking action without discussing overcoming fear. Just reading some of this section may have brought fear to your mind thinking about taking a signifi- cant step forward. That is understandable because these may be very new and challenging steps for you. I will also say that to be fearful is not acceptable. I know that sounds strong, but that is straight from God. We are made to sense and feel things in this life. Fear is in us from birth to help protect us. However, God does not allow fear to be part of our make-up to prevent us from walking in faith. For many people, that is exactly what happens: fear hinders their faith.

You have probably heard many definitions of fear over the years, and many people may have tried to convince you of how to get past it. Ultimately, fear is a feeling. The general way we become fearful is to let something into our thinking. We start to logically consider it, then become emotional about it one way or another. The emotion could be excitement about doing something new that is pushing us out of our comfort zones. This causes our brains to produce serotonin, endorphins, oxytocin, and dopamine, all of which help propel us forward. When we choose to focus on fear, we create a brain chemical called glutamate, which pulls us back. We have a choice about how we handle every process and situation in life. God says so.

I used to deal with fear so much that it drove me to ponder taking drastic measures. Through the years, I have learned to depend on God's truth and talk to Him about what is right and wrong and where to place my focus. However, only up until about six years ago did I still deal with at least a small challenge of fear, then God had me focus on Joshua 1:9-10, which says, "Have I not commanded you? Be strong and courageous. Do not be afraid or discouraged for the Lord your God will be with you wherever you go." You may notice in that scripture that God didn't recommend or advise. He didn't just make a good suggestion. God commanded. I realized that if God has made this command, and if I choose to disobey it, I am then choosing to sin.

I committed that day to shift my mind to God and His truth whenever my thinking started to go down the road of fear. It was not easy, especially at first, but it has now become second nature for me. I don't have time for fear in my life if I am going to pursue everything God wants me to. There is a great anonymous quote that says, "Worry is like a rocking chair; it gives you something to do but gets you nowhere." The choice is up to each one of us to live our lives or waste them by worrying.

One of those fear situations came up for me about a year after I made the commitment to catch fear as it comes up, turn it over to God, and move on. I was in discussions about leading a new division of coaches in a startup organization. The executive leadership was not completely sold on me being the right person to step up to this next level. As I considered how to respond, I felt God put into my mind, "I am giving this to you. You must take it." I knew I had to be bold, be confident, and stand on God's promises. I did! Four years later, I was overseeing a staff of nearly 200 employees that were impacting hundreds of thousands of other people.

One final thing I will share comes from my specialized training in an area that was designed to support our sales team. We would be brought into finalist meetings with key prospective customers to demonstrate what we do and how we do it. Ideally, this would lead to getting a new customer for our product. In one training, an instructor told me that going into these meetings with Fortune 500 companies will increase nervousness. He said that it is normal. The decision then becomes what you do with the stress. It is like a razor's edge. If you fall on one side of the edge you are letting fear take root, and it will cause you to stumble and make mistakes. If, however, you accept that nervous energy with its heightened senses and acute awareness and allow it to propel you to step up your game, you will be very successful. I chose the second option and had very successful demos with leaders of some of the largest and most successful companies in our country. You also have that choice with anything that comes up in life that puts you on the razor's edge to decide on faith or fear. Choose God and choose faith. There is no greater life to live.

DO NOT STOP THROWING

Kurt Warner grew up in the town of Cedar Falls, Iowa. He played several sports, but shined on the football field. Several major football schools recruited him, but none of them offered him a scholarship because they doubted Kurt would be a success in Division One football. He signed up for school and played at the University of Northern Iowa, which is where he was the backup quarterback until his senior year. When he finally got to play, he had a fantastic senior year and was named Conference Offensive Player in 1993.

Kurt was drafted by the Green Bay Packers after his senior year, but had a very rough time at training camp. His style was different from what the Packers were used to, and they even gave him the nickname "Pop Warner", referencing an old NFL football coach who stayed around too long. The Packers cut Warner from the team and he went home to be with his wife Brenda and their kids.

Kurt had to find a way to make a living, but at the same time not give up his commitment to pursue his dream. He went to work for the Cedar Falls Hy-Vee Food Store, stocking shelves for minimum wage, one of the most humbling experiences of his life. It is reported that even during this time he kept working on his throwing and other football skills to prepare for his next opportunity. In 1995, he was signed by the Iowa Barnstormers, a team in the Arena Football League. He led his team to two Arena Bowl appearances in those following years.

Kurt was scheduled for a tryout with another NFL team in 1997, but during his honeymoon, he was bitten on his throwing arm by a poisonous spider and could not go. He never gave up, and four years after being cut from the Packers, he became the backup quarterback for the St. Louis Rams. Kurt got his chance to play only because the starting and backup quarterbacks were both injured at the start of the season. Even the head coach said he hoped Kurt could hold the team together and win one or two games until one of the other quarterbacks could play.

And win, he did! He led the Rams to a 13-3 record that year. They went all the way to the Super Bowl and in 1999 Kurt played in Super Bowl XXXIV in front of 72,000 fans and 800,000,000 TV viewers. With two minutes left, the game was tied when Kurt threw the touchdown pass that earned him the Most Valuable Player award and a Super Bowl Championship ring. He had one of the greatest seasons a quarterback has ever had in the NFL. Not only did he become known for his commitment to pursue his dream, but also for his dedication to his family, a clean lifestyle, and his Christian faith. You can read more about this story in his autobiography *Keep Your Head Up*.

Bible Verse:

Philippians 4:13 (NIV) – "I can do all things through Christ who strengthens me."

Prayer:

Dear Jesus, I love you, I thank you, and I praise you for loving me and saving me. You are my Lord. I always plan to do what is right and follow you, but sometimes I don't. Please help me to focus only on you and to take action when you call me to. The result is not up to me, but up to you, so help me to be obedient and follow you always. In the Name of Jesus, Amen.

Take Action:

1. What is one thing you believe God wants you to take action on?
2. Will you commit to God right now to take action (yes or no)? If yes, when and how will you do it? I recommend you write down your commitment and share it with someone.

Additional Resources:

Book - *If You Want to Walk on Water, You've Got to Get Out of the Boat* by John Ortberg

Movie – *Luther* Produced by Brigitte Rochow, Alexander Thies, Christian P. Stehr

Music – "So Will I" ("100 Billion X") by Hillsong United

Tool - *The Performance Planner* by Zig Ziglar at www.ziglar.com

CHAPTER 8
BUILD WALLS

C hapter Focus: *As a Christian, you are responsible to control certain thoughts and actions in order to glorify God and have fullness of life. Without that control, you cannot follow God well because there is always something tripping you up. You can easily get into a cycle of being tripped up by the same thing over and over, which prevents you from experiencing peace and victory. This chapter will focus on the importance of self-control and self-discipline. God requires this in certain areas of your life in order to hear, know, and follow Him daily. Lack of self-control may be hindering and preventing you from maturing into the person God wants you to be. Don't worry; if God asks you to do something, He will help you do it. This chapter will help you know what He asks you to control in your life as well as how to ask Him to help you, and will grow your walk with Him.*

THE PARROT

There is a story about a man who went to a pet store one day to look for a dog, but found this beautiful and amazing parrot. The parrot seemed kind and well-spoken, so the man decided to purchase the parrot instead.

Once he got the parrot home, he found out that this bird was the exact opposite of well-behaved. The parrot literally had no self-control, and the more the man tried to correct him, the worse it got. The parrot spoke very loudly and abusively. He was full of vulgarities and never listened. He would fly around knocking things over in the house, and by the fourth day, the man had had it. He took the parrot back to the store only to find out there was a three-day return policy. Now he was stuck.

The owner of the store suggested giving the parrot treats to reward good behavior. Once at home, the parrot acted well only one time, then snatched the whole bag of treats from the owner's hand and ate them all. The parrot just simply could not control himself and the owner could not control him, either.

The owner grabbed the parrot, opened the freezer, threw him in and shut the door. There was banging and smashing and swearing. But after 30 seconds all was calm. There was no noise. The owner then felt horrible. He only wanted to scare the parrot, not kill it. Frantically he opened the freezer and slowly the parrot walked out onto his owner's arm. He was visibly shaken up and clearly changed. He was proper, respectful, and very courteous.

The owner was shocked as the parrot said, "I am so sorry for all of the trouble I have caused you. I was completely in the wrong. I have had a full change of heart and I will forever respect you. Whatever you request, I will do it. Please do forgive me." The owner was amazed and accepted the bird's apology. Then the bird politely asked, "May I ask just one more question kind, sir? Please, could you tell me, what did the chicken do?"

Thankfully God does not throw us into a freezer to discipline us. The term "self-control" is self-explanatory. We are required by God to take responsibility for our thoughts, our words, and our actions. Many thoughts go through our minds, as well as many choices we are responsible to make on a daily basis. However, many of the options we could choose in life are not what would bring us closer to God or His purpose. Self-control not only means doing the right things in this life, it also means avoiding doing the wrong things. When you choose to follow Jesus, right and wrong are defined by His Word!

A verse that clearly shows the juxtaposition between what we some-times want to do and what we should do is Galatians 5:16-18 (NIV). It says, "So I say, walk by the Spirit, and you will not gratify the desires of the flesh. For the flesh desires what is contrary to the Spirit, and the Spirit what is contrary to the flesh. They are in conflict with each other so that you are not to do whatever you want. But if you are led by the Spirit, you are not under the law."

God does not control us. God gives us His Word and His Spirit to direct us. The choice is ours. All day every day, we are constantly presented with options. We can choose God's way, the world's way, our own way, or even Satan's way.

CONTROL

I obviously misnamed this chapter. This is a Christian book. Who in his right mind would talk about building walls when the very foundation of Christianity is about love and tearing down walls to show Jesus to others? It sounds strange to name a chapter "Build Walls", especially when the previous chapter talks about faith. Stay with me, because the chapter is not misnamed--it just may not be what you think it is.

If you remember, Truth 9 in Chapter 2 says, **"You must grow and mature"** as a Christian. 2 Peter 1:5-8 (NIV) goes with this truth and says, "For this very reason, make every effort to add to your faith goodness; and to goodness, knowledge; and to knowledge, self-control; and to self-control, perseverance; and to perseverance, godli-ness; and to godliness, mutual affection; and to mutual affection, love. For if you possess these qualities in increasing measure, they will keep you from being ineffective and unproductive in your knowledge of the Lord Jesus Christ."

The fourth step in the verse above is where Christians really get tripped up. There are many things God asks us to do, and not do, as followers of Jesus. When we become Christians, God does not just take over our lives, reprogram our brain, and cause all of our actions to be holy. What He does do is gives us a way to communicate with Him through prayer, provides His written Word, and interacts with us through the Holy Spirit. These three supports help us discern what is right and what is wrong in life. The Holy Spirit also gives us the strength to actually do what is right.

To help clarify, here are the three main persons of God:

1. God the Father is the creator of the universe. He is the one who chose to make everything. He sent His Son Jesus to come to this earth and show us how to live.
2. Jesus is the very Word of God. God made all of His creation through His spoken word and that spoken Word literally is Jesus. Before he came as a human being, He was the Word of God the Father who put everything into place.
3. The Holy Spirit is the Spirit of God. We all have a spirit within our being and the Holy Spirit is the third part of God that comes into our lives when we ask Jesus to come into our hearts. The Holy Spirit leads us to God's plan and truth.

To put it another way, God, in three persons, is the designer, creator, and controller of the universe. His Word is so powerful that it literally created everything we see, including you. We cannot comprehend the power of God, but when He says something, it is! There is no question nor challenge. His promises are always true and correct. He is the ultimate authority.

God promises to give you, as a follower of Jesus, fullness of life on this earth (John 10:10) and eternity with Him (John 3:16). He proclaims that He loves you (1 John 3:1), that He is with you now and will always be with you (Deuteronomy 31:6). He confirms that He has a good plan for you (Jeremiah 29:11). God says He will work all things together for good, even the things that seem bad (Romans 8:28). There are many other promises that God makes that you can absolutely count on to be true. What you do with His promises is up to you! Even as a Christian, you have the choice to believe them, act upon them, and experience these promises in your life. You also have the choice to ignore what God says and choose your own path.

Self-control, the key to Christian maturity, is one of the requirements and results of really following God through the power of the Holy

Spirit. Galatians 5:22 (NIV) says – "But the fruit of the Spirit is love, joy, peace, forbearance, kindness, goodness, faithfulness, gentleness, and self-control." We have to have enough self-control to listen to God and His leading in order to get more self-control from the Holy Spirit. Here is why. God set up this world, and our lives, to work in a certain way. He knows exactly how we should live in order to have the things He desires for us in this life.

Self-control is about your willingness to surrender everything--and I mean everything--to God and then live the way He asks you to do. It is about doing what He leads you to do and loving the way God loves. Just like driving on that road, if you decide instead to go the wrong direction, drive recklessly, or not pay attention, you may end up in a ditch--or worse, in the hospital or dead--and not experience all God has for you.

Here are some definitions to get us started (from www.lexico.com powered by Oxford).

1. Self-control – The ability to control oneself, in particular, one's emotions and desires or the expression of them in one's behavior, especially in difficult situations.
2. Self-discipline – The ability to control one's feelings and overcome one's weaknesses; the ability to pursue what one thinks is right despite temptations to abandon it.

These attributes are required to follow God, and sometimes they are not easy to do. Both are necessary in order to "grow up" in our faith. The main difference between self-control and self-discipline is that self-control is reactive while self-discipline is proactive. Self-control means you control yourself in your responses, your words, and your thinking as life happens. It determines whether you will do what God wants you to do in situations that arise or if you will follow your own emotions, will, and pride (such as when someone cuts you off in traffic). Self-discipline means you are deciding ahead of time to do something (such as read the Bible each morning) and stick to doing it even though you are tempted not to follow through.

On one hand, with self-control, you respond to things that happen to you in a Godly way. On the other hand, with self-discipline, you are also making commitments to new actions you will take to follow God. They are both critical to you fully living out your purpose by faith in God.

As we live as God directs us, the pieces of our lives work together for Him. We also have peace in our hearts when we are in right standing with God, which is called holiness. We can hear him speak to us. When we do not have self-control, we are bounced around in life like a boat on the waves, trying to get somewhere but never fully able to gain control and move forward. Many times, we cannot even hear God because of the frequent storms of life and the fear they bring.

The bedrock key to self-control is spending time with God every day. When you take the initiative and make the time to keep this commitment, God will then help you in every other area of your life. Instead of being bashed by the storm, Jesus will calm the wind and waves. In your home and in your heart there will be peace and confidence that only comes from Him.

WALLS

Here is how important self-control is. Proverbs 25:28 (NIV) says "Like a city whose walls are broken down is a person who lacks self-control." To give perspective, back when this Proverb was written, there were no tanks, or guns, or planes. There was no modern technology for war. It was swords and spears and hand-to-hand combat. It required bows and arrows and catapults. Therefore, what a city needed to protect itself were big, strong walls. With this type of fortress and military men guarding the perimeter atop the wall, the city was safe and secure. Without walls, the enemy could come in at any time and take over the city and destroy it.

This is an analogy for your life. This Proverb is saying that self-control (self-discipline) in your life is like those walls around the city. Without them, your enemy (the devil) can come right into your life and wreak havoc and even destroy it. Even though you are a Christian and trust in God, for you to mature and be safe in Him, you must have self-control to protect you and stay close to Him.

Like walls for the city, you need walls in your life, as well. Not physical walls, per se, but mental and spiritual walls. In other words, instead of getting physically attacked like the city in the analogy above, you are getting attacked daily and even hourly in your mind. The evil one in this world constantly works on getting you to believe lies and deception with a goal of getting you to act against what God asks and promises. Even worry, doubt, and fear are actions against God. This is because you are believing lies and deceptions that have snuck through or over your wall.

Here is the most extreme example I can think of. In Matthew chapter 4, Jesus was getting ready to start his ministry and just before doing that, he was led by the Spirit into the wilderness for 40 days. During this time, he ate no food. Verse 2 has to be the most downplayed comment in the Bible, which says, "After fasting for 40 days and nights, He was hungry."

Are you kidding me! It just says, "He was hungry." I would have been ready to eat my own arm. I probably would have been close to death, or I at least would have acted like it. If I were God, which we all should be glad I am not, I would have had Matthew write something quite dramatic like "After 40 days, Jesus was near starvation with no energy left and was ready to die, yet he still trusted God when he was tempted." I digress. The point is that "hungry" is a huge understatement.

At this time, at Jesus' weakest moment, the Devil came to him and tempted him with many things. Notice that the devil did not beat him, push him, or rob him. He tempted him by asking questions, offering worldly seductions, and trying to make deals with Jesus that were against God's truth. He was attacking the city walls of Jesus' spirit and soul. He was trying to make him drive off the road God the Father had set him on and go over a cliff by giving into urges instead of following God.

Jesus defended against these attacks by quoting God's truth. He stopped the attacks before they could penetrate into his heart and soul by quoting scripture that was straight from God. He knew the truth and stood on it. After his success against the assault that came against the very walls of his soul, he started his ministry. This is our battle, also!

It is unlikely that you will be led into the desert by God or asked to fast for 40 days and nights and then be tempted directly by the devil. However, it is very likely that every day, you will be presented with options and decisions that are not from God. These include things like lust, temptation, worry, doubt, fear, anger, and similar things. You have to make right choices moment by moment that will lead to strong walls and great defense of your mind. If you make poor choices, your walls will break down and allow the enemy to keep coming in and wreaking havoc.

Unfortunately, you may not even be aware that this breaking down of walls is happening on a daily basis. It is easy to feel as if you have been given a bad deal, life is unfair, and there is nothing that can be done, which is a solid lie. It goes back to the fourth step in maturity, which is knowing what discipline you need, then putting it into place by living according to God's truth and plan. Following the fourth step creates the true walls of your mind to guard against the evil one.

The great news is that Satan cannot force his way through, around, or over your wall. You control access to your life. Picture it this way: consider that your mind (your logic, will, and emotions) has a huge wall of protection around it. There is a gate that opens and closes to your mind to let things in or to block them out, and you are in charge of that gate. You have to determine if each thing approaching that gate is good (from God) or bad (from the enemy). This seems simple, but your enemy is a master deceiver and will figure out any and every strategy to penetrate those city walls.

The gate to your mind that I am talking about is your decision-making. The only way you will know if you should open that gate up to a thought or idea is by knowing God's truth and will, then using His wisdom. If you do not know what God wants and promises, you will let anything through that gate. This includes what feels good, what looks good, what you think should worry you, things that will hurt other people, etc.

It may seem as if we are spending an inordinate amount of time on this wall and gate idea. We are, because this is what determines your very life! You are the decider of what you believe, what you let in, and what you act upon. God has set up everything for you to be joyful, prosperous, and successful according to His plan. You are responsible to build the walls, secure the gate, and have self-discipline in the areas He calls you to. He will help you, but you must make the choice and take action.

THE ENEMY

Attacks from the enemy will come. It's not a question of "if" but "when", which is usually daily. You need a fortress around your mind to protect it. You need a wall of truth to defend against the arrows of deception from the enemy and swords of temptation and doubt. You must have the self-control to put up this wall in your mind. God will help you so that, as Jesus promises in John 8:32 (NIV), "you shall know the truth, and the truth will set you free". The solid wall of truth, wisdom, and knowledge is a strong fortress against the lies, doubts, and temptations of your enemy.

As a side note, if you don't believe in the need to guard your mind and your life, here is the picture of what you're up against. 1 Peter 5:8-11 (NIV) says, "Be alert and of sober mind. Your enemy the devil prowls around like a roaring lion looking for someone to devour. Resist him, standing firm in the faith, because you know that the family of believers throughout the world is undergoing the same kind of suffering. And the God of all grace, who called you to his eternal glory in Christ, after you have suffered a little while, will himself restore you and make you strong, firm, and steadfast. To Him be the power forever and ever. Amen."

You are up against a lion looking to devour you. There is a spiritual destroyer after your soul, your mind, and your very life, but don't worry. You can stand up against Him because you are called to be self-controlled by resisting him and standing firm in the faith. That is your part of the obligation. God's obligation is that He will restore you to make you strong, firm, and steadfast. The only way to grow strong in your life and faith is to stand firm on God's truth.

How does this enemy, the lion, try to destroy you? Galatians 5:19-25 (NIV) describes it this way – "The acts of the flesh are obvious: sexual immorality, impurity, and debauchery, idolatry and witchcraft, hatred, discord, jealousy, fits of rage, selfish ambition, dissensions, factions, and envy; drunkenness, orgies and the like. I warn you, as I did before, that those who live like this will not inherit the kingdom of God. But the fruit of the spirit is love, joy, peace, forbearance, kindness, goodness, faithfulness, gentleness, and self-control. Against such things, there is no law. Those who belong to Christ have crucified the flesh with its passions and desires. Since we live by the Spirit, let us keep in step with the Spirit."

Here are two key points from these verses. The first is that in God's eyes there is definitely good and bad, holy and evil, and right and wrong. He does not have the worldview so prevalent today, which is believing that everyone can have his or her own truth and as long as you feel it's right then it must be right. The second is that we are responsible to choose between right and wrong each and every day. God will not force you to learn His way or to do the right thing. You have to choose to know His Word (the Bible) and seek Him in prayer, then follow. He is willing and able to walk with you day by day and hour by hour to show you the way.

SOFTWARE

I will never forget a day at work many years ago when a co-worker sent me an interesting message. I don't remember the subject line of the email, but I sure remember what it did. Once I opened it, a horrible warning came up, then I could see all the files on my hard drive and one by one they were getting deleted in quick fashion. I tried canceling and deleting the operation and nothing worked. I tried to shut the computer down with no luck.

My heart sank as I watched this all unfold. I knew there were several huge problems with this situation. The first is that someone got into my computer and it was compromised. The second was that all my files and hard work could be gone, or at minimum, tough to retrieve. Third, my employer would not be very happy with me if the email actually destroyed my computer system.

All these thoughts went through my head; thirty seconds felt like an eternity. My files were gone. My hard work and dedication were erased. My head spun as I tried to figure out what to do. Should I just resign now? As I watched the screen, a final message popped up letting me know this was all a joke and that I had been duped. I was in shock.

I cannot count all of the emotions that went through my mind and body. I was elated that all of this was a farce and that all of my files were still there. I was also ready to wring someone's neck because whoever the evil person was who did this needed to pay. I felt virtually every emotion known to man during the short time after discovering this heart-stopping joke.

That situation caused enough alarm in my life that I made some immediate changes. Although this was a simple joke, it could have been real. I began to double and triple-check anything questionable coming into my inbox before opening it. I made sure with our IT team that my virus protection was up to date and working all the time. I also confirmed that all of my files were backed up and continually being backed up to ensure I would never lose everything. This also taught me to do the same things with my home computer systems.

Chances are that you have a computer or use one at work. Even if you don't, you realize the importance of protecting them. There is far too much valuable information that criminal minds can get to by hacking into personal devices and servers. They can wreak havoc and cause fear. The big question for all of us is why do we guard technology more than our own minds?

Let's compare your mind with my computer. The operating system of a computer like the one I am typing on now determines its actions. As the user (in this case, me) types on it, the keyboard and mouse perform specific actions. It is an amazing machine.

You also have control over your mind and as you think various thoughts and make decisions. Your body then carries out the function of your brain to act on purpose. Like the computer, there are evil plots in this world to try and infiltrate your mind, just like getting into your computer, to corrupt it. Then your actions, words, and thoughts would follow.

Your mind is much more powerful and valuable than any software ever created or that will ever be created. It is even more important that you guard it with the right "virus protection", effective security, and accurate information. Unfortunately, most people put much more time, effort, and investment into protecting their computer brains than they do their own human brains.

Self-control is deciding in your life that you will guard the greatest asset you have, which is your brain (your heart, soul, and mind). There is a greater backup system, virus control, and safeguard for your brain than will ever be invented for computers. It is our creator, programmer, and protector--God in three persons.

You may have had a major scare in life. It is not too late to take your life seriously, to put in the greatest brain protection available in the universe. If you are willing, He is willing to help you. God is the God of yesterday, today, and forever. You must choose to learn and apply the key principles of self-control and self-discipline that will keep the software of your very being strong, fully functioning, protected, and backed up.

Don't let a scare become a nightmare. Your enemy is the greatest human mind-hacker in history, and he knows and follows your tendencies until he finds a way in. You are fighting a battle you cannot see, yet you are assured victory if you choose to actually follow God, not just in thought, but also in action.

In the next chapter, we will cover how and in which areas to exercise self-discipline, but the question you must ask yourself right now is whom you will serve. Will you serve this world, the enemy, or your own personal desires and be bound up like a hostage just like my computer--or will you choose to serve the One who sets you free?

This is the very question Joshua asked the people of Israel when leading them into the promised land and the freedom of God. Joshua 24:14-15 (NIV): "Now, therefore, fear the Lord and serve him in sincerity and in faithfulness. Put away the gods that your fathers served beyond the river and in Egypt and serve the Lord. And if it is evil in your eyes to serve the Lord, choose this day whom you will serve…as for me and my house, we will serve the Lord."

HOW TO APPLY SELF-CONTROL

Most of us would love to use better self-control in life. We all struggle with this to different extents and will do so until the day we leave this earth. While we are here, the world has so many things pulling at our attention, thoughts, emotions, and desires that it becomes work to stay the course God has for us. We might even believe that there are things other than God that we need to have or do in this life in order to live fully or even be happy.

To illustrate: I remember many years ago, a friend of mine--I will call her Amanda--made an amazing statement. She emphatically said to me, "I can control a lot of things in my life, but if there is chocolate around, I have to eat it." I was taken aback. I get the chocolate rage, but does she literally "have to eat it?" I was tempted to lock her in a See's chocolate candy store for 30 minutes and see what she would do.

I challenged her exaggerated statement and she pushed right back. She said she literally has to eat chocolate and that she cannot keep herself from doing so. She then made the comment that she would die without it.

At this point, it was good that I was not an evil person. The thought then entered my mind that I should get a one-pound Hershey bar, lock it in a clear encasement that she could not open, then put it on the kitchen table to see what happened. Would she get a hammer or saw to try to destroy the box? Would she literally die without her chocolate?

Thankfully, I actually exercised my own self-control and did not pull this stunt. It is good for two reasons that I didn't. The first is my own health, because she would probably have beaten me with the one-pound bar of chocolate, case and all! The second is her health because she would have found a way to get into the box and eat the whole thing.

Instead, I challenged her thinking by stating that she would not die by avoiding chocolate. As she defended her position, I gave her this analogy. I said that if someone came and tied her to a chair then put chocolate all around her so that she could not get to it but still gave her regular food, she would not literally die. She might be tortured thinking about the taste of chocolate in her mouth and visualizing eating it, but she surely would not die. She finally conceded to that preposterous idea, realizing that her addiction was a choice, not a necessity.

Many times in life, we can believe false things as true. To have self-control in your life that brings God's freedom, peace, and joy, you first have to examine the things you think, say, and do. You must then compare them to what God says is right and true, then make the commitment to change anything that does not agree with His truth.

This is where the rubber meets the road. It is easy to believe God loves you and to choose to love Him. It is easy to learn about God and go to church. It is easy to join a small group and be supported by others. It is even easy to read this book and agree with everything written in it.

It is quite another thing to look at exactly how God wants you to live, think, and love and to compare that to how you currently live, think, and love, and then to change everything in your life that is off track. It takes courage to look closely at yourself and to really see where your heart and motivation lie. It takes courage to say you will live exactly how God calls you to live, in every area of life, to the best of your ability. It takes courage to challenge the negative, fearful, and deeply-ingrained thinking you have considered true all your life and hold it to the light comparing it to what God says in a litmus test.

There is NOTHING in this world or in your life that will master you if you take God at His Word and do what He calls you to do. You can do it! God is with you and will help you. Remember, at the very core of everything God made in this world, including you, is love. God loves you and wants the very best for you in this life and for eternity. He would never ask you to do anything in your life that goes against His love and promises, but you are the deciding factor.

You can choose not to look at certain areas of your life. You can choose not to examine your thought life and the desires of your heart. You can also choose not to live out your full purpose. You can choose to settle for second best and never fully realize what God can do in, to, and through you. By doing this, you will never experience the full freedom and joy in this life that only comes by letting God be the God of your life.

Just like that chocolate addiction story, you can choose to hold onto anything in life other than God, or you can choose to hold on to Him. One choice holds you captive and the other sets you free.

THE CHOICES

You always have a choice. You may not think you do, but that is a lie. You always have a choice to pick your attitude, to pick your thoughts, to pick your actions (or inactions). Sometimes you cannot control what is done to you or the forces around you, but you can choose how you respond to them in your mind, in your words, and in your actions. If we had no choice in these areas, God would not ask us to take control of them. God does not ask you to control the things you cannot control, such as your gender, your race, when or where you were born, your parents, etc. He does call you to control everything you can. You have a choice to be in line with Him.

When it comes to self-control/discipline, there are two things God calls for:

1. Control ourselves to not do things He asks us not to do.
2. To discipline ourselves to do the things He asks us to do.

It's that simple and that hard at the same time. How can you know if you are doing the right things and avoiding the wrong things? My guess is that you already know. You know in your heart, in your mind, and in your spirit if you are disobeying God in one or many areas of your life.

God also may show you something through His Word that you need to change. Here are just a few examples from the Bible that He says are wrong and against Him (Galatians 5:19-20, Colossians 3:5-6):

Sexual immorality – having sex with anyone other than your spouse

Impurity – not in right standing with God

Debauchery – excessive indulgence in pleasure (drunkenness, etc.)

Idolatry (and witchcraft) – having any other god or spiritual focus in your life

Hatred – intense or passionate dislike for someone

Discord – disagreements

Jealousy – state or feeling of being jealous, envious

Fits of rage – violent, uncontrollable anger

Selfish ambition – concerned chiefly with your own personal profit or pleasure

Lust – very strong sexual desire (for someone who is not your spouse)

Other wrongs found in various scriptures: pride, envy, laziness, greed, gluttony, murder, sodomy, oppression of the weak, defrauding, etc.

This is important to understand: none of us is perfect, nor will we ever be while we live on this earth. To provide perspective, when I looked up a list of sins in the Bible, I found 667 with supporting scriptures. It would be nearly impossible to even memorize what they are, much less to avoid every single one of them every day.

There is a big difference between living each day the best way you can according to your faith, exercising self-control and committing unplanned sin, versus doing something regularly and intentionally that is not God's will with no intention of changing it. The first example pleases God. The second example does not.

When you live by faith to do what is right, you please God. When you please God, you are blessed by Him and able to live the purpose for which He made you. You were made to change the world by first changing yourself (with God's help) in any area that does not please Him.

Take 3-5 minutes right now to pray and ask God what, if anything, you need to ask forgiveness for right now. Then ask Him what you need to change in the way you live. This takes courage and self-discipline. Now, ask for forgiveness, through the blood of Jesus, and commit to living the right way.

HOOVER DAM

The Hoover Dam, on the border of Nevada and Arizona, is a marvel to see. It was constructed in the Black Canyon of the Colorado River between 1931 and 1936. It took thousands of workers to build it, hundreds of whom lost their lives. The price to build this amazing structure was $49 million dollars in 1931 which, converted to today's dollars, is $664 million.

The height of this dam is 726 feet, which is over two football fields, and it is 1,244 feet long (over four football fields). The thinnest part of the dam is at the top, which is 45 feet wide, and the thickest at the bottom is 680 feet, which again is over two football fields in thickness.

The purpose of the dam is to generate power, control flooding, and regulate and store water, plus provide a place for recreation. Its construction created Lake Meade, which means it is holding back 247 square miles of water. Standing at the top of this magnificent wall and looking down is awe-inspiring. From the top of the dam you can see Lake Meade, which is full of hundreds of miles of water--all held back by a wall that is over two football fields in height and two football fields thick. The title of this chapter is "Building Walls" and this is the most impressive wall I have ever seen.

The powerful comparison I heard about this particular wall and the walls in our life is that if there were a crack the size of a quarter, the water would start seeping through with increasing strength. In a short period of time, the gigantic wall would come crashing down. The resulting flood waters would cause complete devastation to everything around it. This is why the dam was designed so cautiously and constructed so soundly, and is watched so closely.

In your life, the dam is made up of each area of self-control that God has you put in place to protect you from the evil one. Satan looks for any cracks in those walls. He doesn't need to come in with a sledge-hammer to take the walls down; he just needs to find any little crack in your life to enter, then start seeping through more and more strongly until he brings the wall down and causes calamity. Design, construct, and watch the walls in your life through self-control as God leads you.

Bible Verse:

GALATIAN 5:22-23 (NIV) – "THE FRUIT OF THE SPIRIT IS LOVE, JOY, peace, forbearance, kindness, goodness, faithfulness, gentleness, and self-control. Against such things, there is no law."

Prayer:

Dear Jesus, I want to love you and serve you in all I think, say, and do. I know there are areas of my life where I need better self-control and self-discipline. Please help me, through the power and strength of your Holy Spirit, to put all the right things into place in my life, and remove anything that is not of you. Lead me and I will follow. In Jesus' name, Amen!

Take Action:

1. What are the things I struggle with in life?
2. In which of these things is God asking me to exert self-control?

Additional Resources:

Book - *If You Want to Walk on Water, You've Got to Get Out of the Boat* – by John Ortberg

Movie – *Fireproof* – By Mark Burnett and Roma Downey

Music – "So Will I (100 billion X)" by Hillsong United

Tool - Win With God Today at www. madetochangetheworld.com / resources

CHAPTER 9
BE STRONG

C hapter Focus: *Life can get very hard at times. This world can have a heavy impact on us, and were we left to ourselves, it would be devastating. However, Jesus our Lord and Savior says that you are His, that He is with you always, and that He has overcome the world. So, what are we to do when the heavy winds and waves of life are striking us and trying to beat us down? The answer is to stay the course by continuing to do what God has called us to do in the first place until He shows us something different. We are to persevere, and in the process, we will become more like Jesus. This chapter is all about how to be strong in Him through the hard times, what to do to persevere, and how to not only get through the trials, but become stronger because of them.*

THE BEAR

When tough times come, there are different ways to handle them. You can shrink back and be overcome, or you can be the overcomer. Here is the story of two guys, each one having a different mindset when facing a major struggle.

Two buddies were out camping in the woods and having a great time. A couple of days into the trip, they saw a bear in the distance approaching quickly. They both felt terror and looked at each other wondering what to do. The first man froze. He was stuck because his desperate feelings began to overtake him.

The other man thought quickly. He took off as fast as he could for their tent and started putting on his running shoes. The other man, still completely alarmed, shouted at his friend, saying, "What are you doing? You can't outrun that bear!" Confidently, the second man finished tying his shoes and started to run. Without breaking his pace, he shouted to the man who was frozen, "I don't have to outrun the bear; I just have to outrun you!" Apparently, they weren't great friends!

KEEP GOING AND LEARNING

A couple of years ago, I found myself writing some important words to help me remember life's priorities. As we get older, we let many things shape our thoughts and ambitions, which pulls us off track. We also let disappointments, worries, and fears shape us. In order to keep the important aspects as my priority, I wrote these words:

"Love like it's your last day,

Learn like a newborn,

Live life on purpose,

Lead with passion."

We already shared that love needs to be our primary focus in life. We also discussed the importance of living our purpose. As we walk close to God, which is the foundation of this book, a passionate life is a result. Now, let's focus on learning like a newborn. As I am sure you have already gathered, I think our daughter Ellie is pretty amazing. I am sure all parents think their young ones are pretty special, too. What is incredible with every child is how they learn and grow on a daily basis.

At three years, Ellie's vocabulary is pretty extensive. She can explain herself quite well – sometimes too well! She went from just speaking a few words a year ago to now having full interactions.

Her latest trick is to balance herself on one leg and then jump around the house. Apparently, this is something most kids do around the age of four, and not three, just to add to my "holy bragging". She literally just started trying this a week ago and now is quite steady and even switches legs. She then started challenging me to stand on one leg for 10 seconds to see who loses their balance first. Thankfully, I am still winning this little game.

The point is that Ellie cannot help but learn and grow daily. She never stops stretching herself. She wanted to walk. When she turned one year old she kept trying and falling, then trying again. She then got it and soon afterward learned to run. She learned all the letters before age two and could pick all of them out of books. Now she is learning to write. She genuinely has fun learning and makes it a game.

You probably learned just like this growing up. Have you stopped growing like this? Unfortunately, we easily start getting into a limited mindset. We begin to think about life based on what we have been told by other people, tough experiences, fear, and our own discouraging self-talk. We start to operate out of fear, not faith. We get stuck in what we believe based on what we "know" and past experiences.

We were not meant to stop learning and growing. We were meant to have an unlimited growth mindset. In the early days, God would walk with Adam and Eve to show them new things. Every day was about learning and growing.

God wants you to learn and grow, and to be excited about what is to come. You may have already formed opinions about this world or about yourself. You may think you already know the limits of what you can and cannot do. Remember my personality test? I was literally told dozens of things I would never be able to do in life, but God had a different plan. He led me to pursue every one of those things through His Holy Spirit and gave me His wisdom and strength.

As you follow God, become like a child again in your faith. Be willing to learn and grow. Become all that God made you to be. You do not know everything right now. As a matter of fact, you know very little of all there is to know, and some of it may even be inaccurate.

To fully live life, you must have a childlike heart. You must be willing to trust, try, and grow. Be curious about what God will show you instead of living in a self-imposed box. To have all that God wants for you, you cannot close your mind. You must open your thinking to the greatness of God. He will teach you and do great things through you if you are willing to learn.

For a moment, think like a child. When was the last time you played on a playground? Mine was a few weeks ago. Ellie loves the playground, so I take her and jump on the swing next to her. It is freeing! I still feel it in my stomach when I start going high. I also climb the miniature rock wall with her, go down the slide, and get into the big plastic boat. I do it all and feel like a kid again.

Regardless of how old your body is, don't limit the kid inside. There is a part of you that longs to have fun, be free, and learn. You were made to be stretched, challenged, and changed. Will you let God do that in you? That is the way to truly live and not just exist.

THINKING IS KEY

In the book *Mindset*, Carol S. Dweck describes the attitudes of our minds as either fixed or growth-oriented. Those with a fixed mindset believe that one statement, one test result, or one personality profile determines who they are. They also believe that one failure shows them to be a failure in life, so they do everything possible to avoid failure and try to be immediately successful in whatever they do. When something does not go their way, they blame others, say they didn't try hard, or abruptly take their ball and go home.

Conversely, the growth mindset does not consider any specific event or result to be the determinant of their future. They believe that learning and growing can make all the difference in what results next. They believe we are continually in the process of growing and learning. They do not become stagnant because of one event, one test, or one pronouncement by another person.

If you believe only in what you know so far in your walk with God, you will be very limited in life. You will have a fixed mindset, and by living this way, you are telling God He is wrong. The truth is you should be actively in the process of growing every day. As soon as you begin to believe you are stuck, you are. Although God has everything you need to do great things through Him, your belief determines the extent of what He can do in your life.

Because of my limited beliefs earlier in life, I was headed for drug abuse or suicide. Years of thinking negatively, holding grudges, and believing what others said about me led me to an inaccurate assessment of myself. I got stuck in believing I should only do things that would boost my confidence and make me look better. I never gave things my all so I could easily blame any failure on not really trying. I hedged my bets to make sure I would never really fail because I never really tried. The problem with my philosophy was that I wasn't really living for God; I was self-preserving.

We all fail at things. If you take the view that those failures define you, you will be stuck. You will become overly cautious, if not paranoid, as you move through life with a focus on preventing failure from ever happening again. On the contrary, if you view life as a child of God, you will learn and grow every day. Failure is not a person (you); it is simply an event to teach you. As you walk in faith, you will see what God can do through you, regardless of your past.

This relates to the second big sticking point in our spiritual maturity as described in 2 Peter 1:5-6, "For this very reason, make every effort to add to your faith goodness; and to goodness, knowledge; and to knowledge, self-control; and to self-control, perseverance; and to perseverance, godliness." The first area where we tend to get stuck is the area of self-control, which we covered in the last chapter. The second area is perseverance. In modern times, most people try to avoid difficult situations at all costs. The new mindset is that if something doesn't feel good, change it; don't even consider struggling through, because that is too painful. If you don't feel good in your marriage, get a divorce. If you don't like the way things are going at work, quit. If finances become too difficult, file bankruptcy. There may be situations where God really wants us to move on, but many times we give up based on feelings and not faith. The problem is that sometimes the struggle may be the very thing God is using to help you grow.

An example of this comes from my career in coaching. The traditional, non-Christian life coach helps people determine what they want in life, then helps them set goals to achieve it. The coach holds the person accountable for success. The driving factor in these coaching conversations is whatever the client wants in order to feel good. Success becomes the agenda. The problem is that this is based solely on the client's own feelings and desires. These can change quickly when not built on God. They can also change directions like the wind, especially when things get hard. The client's focus is not based on truth, but on feelings.

Christian coaching realizes that when someone is pursuing God, hard times may come in the middle of it. When things get difficult, it doesn't mean life is off track. God uses these trials to grow and change us. When we refuse to take on challenges and go through hard times, we are really refusing to learn and grow because of our comfort. 1 Peter 1:6-7 says:

"In all this, you greatly rejoice, though now for a while you may have had to suffer grief in all kinds of trials. These have come so that the proven genuineness of your faith – of greater worth than gold, which perishes even though refined by fire – may result in praise, glory, and honor when Jesus Christ is revealed."

Your important choice in life is between wanting only what *feels* good and what really *is* good. Not everything that happens in life is good. Many things are bad and against God's will. However, if you follow God and not feelings, the promise is this: "God works all things together for good for those who love Him and are called according to His purpose," Romans 8:28-29. Your choice is to believe this promise (or not) in the way you live your life.

ASSESSMENT FOR THE LEARNER'S MIND

Here is a short assessment to see how faithful you are during life's challenges. In this book or on a piece of paper, rank from 1-5 your answer (1 for never/5 for always):

I always turn to God when things get rough in life.

I believe God will work all my struggles together for good.

I can change.

I can learn new things.

I take full responsibility for my own decisions and attitude.

God is in control.

It is my responsibility to learn in order to become more like Jesus.

I look at situations with faith rather than fear.

There is a purpose for struggle in this life.

All struggles in life have spiritual implications.

Total:

If you scored 46 – 50, then you face problems with the right focus.

If you scored 40 – 45, then you generally have the right focus with some areas to grow.

If you scored 30 - 39, then you have growth areas for facing life's problems.

If you scored less than 30, then you profoundly struggle with life's challenges.

THE CATERPILLAR

I heard a story years ago about a boy fascinated by a caterpillar. He noticed it for days, and after a while, the squiggly caterpillar began to cocoon. The transformation captured the boy's attention. Every day he would check it out to see what was happening. At one point, the struggle he watched was so great that the boy couldn't take it anymore, so he snipped part of the cocoon and out came the pupa. The partially formed butterfly laid there for a while, but then quickly died.

The struggle the boy could not bear to continue to watch was the very process the caterpillar **had** to endure to be formed into a beautiful butterfly. I tell this story because we go through many struggles in our own lives, and change is hard. It requires struggle. Sometimes it is messy and makes no sense. It can feel painful or insurmountable, yet, like the caterpillar, if the challenge is not allowed to happen, neither is the growth.

Instead of trying to avoid uncomfortable challenges, take them to God. Ask Him if you are where you should be right now. Ask God if you are doing what He wants you to do. Sometimes you are doing the wrong thing or are in the wrong spot. He will help you move on when that is the case. Other times, you are right where He wants you because of the impact you will make or the change that will occur. Don't be afraid to face the challenge, persevere, and grow. Only God knows what you will become after the breakthrough!

THE MAKING OF A STAR

From the first chapter in Genesis, we know that God made the earth, the sun, and the moon. He made the stars and all of creation. When He made humans, it was His greatest creation because we are made in His image. As He purposefully created us as His masterpiece, He has built within each of us an amazing potential. We can only realize it by following Him closely. We must believe in the truth of becoming the shining star He desires us to be. You must learn and grow and not stagnate.

One such story of a human star is the story of Wilma Rudolf. Several years ago, Dr. Sloan delivered a speech at the Houston Baptist University, and in that speech detailed some of the massive struggles Wilma faced early in life and the accomplishments that came after following God for many years.

Here is part of her story:

Wilma Rudolph was born in 1940, the twentieth of 22 children in her family. Just that in itself is a huge struggle! I can't imagine the dinner table at the Rudolf residence--not only the size of the table but the challenge of trying to actually get food. Just getting fed through the years must have been a miracle.

Wilma was stricken with polio when she was very young. Although she grew up in poverty and in highly challenging circumstances, her family had a deep Christian faith. They taught her that God had a purpose for her life, even with her polio-stricken body.

The year 1940 may as well have been the Middle Ages for polio patients. Wilma's doctors told her family that she would never walk. Wilma's mother refused to give up. She prayed faithfully and massaged Wilma's legs every day for years. It worked! Wilma eventually improved just enough for the doctors to put her in leg braces. Her mother was still determined that her daughter would walk, and she did not give up praying and massaging every day. She persevered for her daughter in faith.

Wilma was able to walk without the clunky braces by the time she was twelve. She learned from her mother about not giving up and not giving in, and in doing so, picked up running. By the time Wilma was fifteen years old, she started winning races. Then she won so many races, she came to be known as the *Tennessee Tornado* and qualified for the 1956 U.S. Olympic team when she was just 16. That in itself was a miracle.

That year, the team went to Melbourne, Australia for the Olympics, but they didn't do very well. Wilma later confessed that she was so happy to just make the team that she disregarded her training. After seeing how badly her team did in 1956, she could have quit. Instead, she rose to a new level of perseverance and commitment. She decided to train like never before for the 1960 Olympics in Rome. That year, Wilma won three gold medals and became known as the fastest woman on earth.

It is worth highlighting a couple of things from Wilma's story. Not only was she poor and finding her place amongst twenty-one siblings, but she also suffered from polio. Polio is a contagious viral illness that causes nerve damage and leads to paralysis and even death. Back in the mid-1900s, polio was a major problem and most people who got it greatly suffered. Thankfully, it is nearly eradicated in western society, but it still affects children and adults in parts of Asia and Africa. Needless to say, having polio is not a great way to start a track career.

Despite the odds, Wilma never gave up, and neither did her mother. They both persevered through the hardest of times. They kept praying, trusting, massaging, and moving. Theirs was a faith that didn't give up. Wilma's mom fought for her daughter by praying, trusting, and persevering day after day, week after week, month after month, and year after year.

What a miracle that Wilma went on to be called the fastest woman on earth! Even if she had only been able to walk, that would have been a powerful story of faith. But what if Wilma's mom had believed what the doctors originally said? What if Wilma had not trusted God every day? Wilma probably would have ended up permanently handicapped and possibly dying young.

You and I are called to persevere and trust in God by acting in faith, especially through the hard times. That is why perseverance is the second biggest downfall for people who try to live for God. It is easy to doubt and give up. It is easy to back down when things are tough. Anyone can do that, but that is not what a child of God does.

Perseverance is the most powerful way God teaches, grows, and changes us. It is easy to sit on your comfortable couch and read about the struggles of Moses, Noah, or Joseph and how they persevered to see God move; it is quite another thing to live it yourself. If you stay committed to God through every trial and keep your faith in Him, somehow, and in some way, God will work everything together for your good (Romans 8:28).

Grow and learn, especially through the hard times. Wilma did. Jesus did! God created the stars. He also made you, and you are called to shine like a star. Stick with God and trust through the struggles. Philippians 2:14-15 says "Do everything without grumbling or arguing, so that you may become blameless and pure children without fault in a warped and crooked generation. Then you will shine among them like stars in the sky."

WHAT DOES IT MEAN TO PERSEVERE?

Persevering is the realization that you have not yet "arrived". No matter what you know, and who you think you know, God has more to show you. The only way you will spiritually mature is to fully commit to God. This means spending time with God and listening to Him. It means to follow Christ as best you can through both good and bad times. It does not mean that when the going gets tough you try to do it all on your own. It does not mean you avoid tough situations. It means that you are willing to go through the struggle while focusing on God and learning in the process.

You may find this commitment to be the toughest thing you will ever do. The choice to press on and go through it versus turn around and retreat will determine the outcome of the situation and your personal growth. Ask yourself these two questions during the struggle:

1. Do I still trust that God is in control?
2. Will I follow Him regardless of what I see with my own eyes?

The definition of perseverance (from Miriam-Webster Dictionary) is "*Continued effort to do or achieve something despite difficulties, failure, or opposition. The action or condition or an instance of persevering.*" Did you notice the word "condition"? We should all have the condition, as Christians, that defaults to seeking, hearing, trusting, and following God by faith. This should be our condition no matter what is happening in the world around us.

The word used in American Standard and King James versions of the Bible instead of perseverance is "patience". Patience means "*Bearing pains or traits calmly and without complaint, steadfast despite opposition, difficulty, or adversity.*" In today's culture, the goal for many people is to experience pleasure and avoid pain. In God's plan, there are times of struggle, and they will transform you toward godliness if you let them.

HOW TO PERSEVERE

In the year 2007, the US economy started to struggle, and no-one knew just how bad it would get. By 2008, the economy not only started to weaken but was headed for a partial collapse that would impact the world. The real estate market had been over-inflated due to bad lending, mortgage defaults, and inflated home prices. Nearly everyone was impacted by the situation, our family included. I was still doing some coaching at the time and also working together with a few friends and family members in real estate at the time of the collapse, which really hit Claudia and me hard.

By late 2008 we found ourselves moving back to California from Florida, but not in the way I had hoped. I had always thought we would move back, but I had planned it to be because we were financially successful. I even had dreams of living part of the year in California and part in Florida. The exact opposite happened. We not only moved back to a desperate situation, but we also had to move in with Claudia's parents.

At nearly 40 years old, we were well over a hundred thousand dollars in debt and barely surviving. Earlier decisions I had thought were led by God were really just my own ideas. Reminiscent of that desolate day on the beach, this had now become one of the most desperate times of my life.

In addition to the financial strain, there was stress on our marriage. We moved back to California to start over and had no jobs. This put a lot of pressure on me, which then impacted my health. I had burned out my adrenal glands. My hormones became out of balance. I was struggling just to get through the day. Seemingly, everything was falling apart, and we were merely trying to survive. I had no energy and I could not think straight. With the limited energy I had, I continued to do the most important thing - draw close to God.

Each day, I would pray and read my Bible. I asked God for wisdom and strength. Even though I did not feel either of these at the time, I decided I would keep digging into God. Even though I felt that for the rest of my life I would simply exist and not really live, I told God that if that really would be the extent of my future, I would still continue trusting in Him. I knew that in the worst-case, I would one day be in heaven and it would all be better. Imagine me, the Christian Life Coach, getting to this point.

Even though it was discouraging to not afford our own place, staying with my mother- and father-in-law (Luis and Judith Roque) was a great blessing. One day, my mother-in-law challenged me. While I was in my "barely existing" mode, she asked me what promises I was standing on from the Bible. I didn't know what she meant. She went on to explain that God has promises for our lives and we need to know those truths, believe them, and stand on them in faith for our very existence. I had been desperately reading the Bible, but I was not "standing on it".

That day, I started looking for Scriptures about God's purpose and plans for me. He also gave me verses about marriage, career, finances, health, and all areas of life. I started to read them daily and then memorize them. To this day, I have 15 verses that I have memorized and repeat every morning as soon as I wake up. I also have nearly 100 more Scriptures that I quote based on the day of the week. I do not allow my mind to start with the things of this world, such as the news, emails, or anything else. I start by quoting the promises of God, then the rest of my day builds upon that foundation. In addition to the Scriptures, I also repeat my Purpose, Mission, and Vision Statements. God has changed my life through my commitment to spend time with Him, memorize and claim His Word, and conversationally pray.

If you would like to see the list of Scriptures I repeat every morning, see appendix A. Feel free to use them yourself, or find other verses as God leads. I include these Scriptures not to pressure you to memorize them, but to lovingly nudge you to stand faithfully on God's promises as my mother-in-law did for me. If you will commit the very beginning of every day to God, you will find that over time your brain will default to God and to truth instead of lies and fear. You must first plug truth into your mind each day if you want all God has for you.

To continue our story, God took Claudia and me from a desperate situation to nearly debt-free (including our home). He helped us rebuild our relationship and now we have little Ellie. I have a career that is amazing, and I am not even sure how God got me here. My health is at 100 percent due to taking care of my body during those following years the way God desires.

I share my story to encourage you that God is faithful! He is with you ALWAYS. He will never leave you nor forsake you. He will never give up on you. He is ready, willing, and able to lead you and show you the way. Are you faithful to God? Are you ALWAYS turning to Him? Do you ever give up? Are you ready, willing, and able to follow as He guides your steps?

PLEASE DON'T THINK THAT IF YOU DO ALL THESE THINGS, LIFE WILL BE perfect. We will all have trouble in this world (John 16:33). The question is who or what you trust during the troubles. If you really want to grow your faith and be strong, realize that it will not happen by avoiding life's difficulties but through perseverance and standing upon the firm foundation of God's Word, truth, and guidance every single day.

DOT COM

For most people in the western world, the "good life" means sleeping in, lounging around, and having enough money to do whatever they want whenever they want. None of these things in themselves are bad. Unfortunately, none of them by itself fulfills God's purpose. Most people think the "ultimate" spot to attain in life is living in comfort and away from struggles. I believed that myself until a boss of mine told me about an article he read.

He had just read a magazine article giving the account of young multi-millionaires who achieved their success early in life during the dot com era. The dot com boom took place in the 1990s and was based on people creating websites that drew many visitors, gaining broad attention, then selling out to bigger companies or through IPOs for a significant profit. For example, AOL and Yahoo are two of those companies.

When interviewed, there was a common theme found among them. They were asked many questions including what they missed most about the days when they had to work. The answers that most of them gave were consistent. They said, "I miss the struggle."

Strangely enough, those who have "arrived" in life and are able to live the American dream found the very thing they were trying to get away from was the thing they missed most. We are designed to take on, overcome, and grow through struggles. We are not made to shy away from the challenges of life. When you recoil from challenges, you hurt God because the very fabric of your being is designed to be an overcomer who walks by faith in Him. You were created to share about Him and without the tests, you won't be able to "testify" about his faithfulness and goodness.

Your struggle may be tough and seem never-ending but persevere and have faith. Amazingly, God has given you the capacity to go through the struggle and He will do it with you. It will change you and grow you. Don't curse the very thing God uses to mold you to be like Jesus. Jesus himself went through a struggle greater than you and I will ever face, yet he never turned back. *It changed the world.* Now, as you live in relationship with Him, He invites you to do the same.

A good friend of mine named Jen Johnson was not a dot com mogul, but her struggle was that she desperately wanted her husband to accept Jesus and become a Christian. For many years it looked like he was going in the opposite direction. Instead of giving up, she dug into God. Day after day, year and year, and decade after decade she remained faithful, just like Wilma Rudolph's mother did. A little over 20 years later, Rich Johnson accepted Christ into his heart and still lives for God every day. If you ask Jen if the struggle was worth it, without hesitation she would respond with an emphatic, "Yes!"

. . .

PUSHING THE ROCK

Here is a final story to help you through the struggles, challenges, and commitment to living for God. It is obviously a fictional story, but I heard it somewhere many years ago and it has stuck with me ever since.

The story is about a man who, after many years of living for himself, decided to turn his life over to God. He let God know that he would do anything God asked him to do and would faithfully follow Him. Changed by God, the man was ecstatic knowing he was ready to change the world.

God accepted his commitment with open arms and led the man to a large boulder. He asked the man to push on the boulder until getting final instructions. The man was quite puzzled at the request, but since he did just commit to doing anything God asked him to, he agreed to push the boulder.

He pushed and pushed but nothing happened. The rock was way too big. After about an hour, he went back to God and said that he was pushing with all his might, but the huge rock was not moving. But God sent him back to push on the rock some more.

A full day went by and then another as this man continued to push on the boulder. Finally, the man went back to God and said that he was really trying to follow what God said, but was not seeing any progress. He told God that he was getting very tired and asked what he should do now. God reminded the man that He would tell him when it was time to do something different and sent him back to the rock.

The man was getting discouraged but remembered his commitment, so he went back to push the boulder. Day after day he pushed. He pushed during the sun and the rain, sleet, and even during some cold days. He was there for weeks, and even months, but the boulder didn't budge. Finally, the man went back to God and said that although he was committed to following Him no matter what and that he would keep pushing the rock if God really wanted him to, he was seriously wondering what this was all about and proclaimed that he saw absolutely no progress and still could not move the rock.

God reminded the man that he had never asked him to move the rock; he only asked him to push on the rock. He then told the man to take a look at himself. His scrawny form was now full of muscle, strength, and the ability to withstand hardships. Pushing did not move the rock. It changed the man.

Effortlessly, God moved the rock out of the way and then showed the man what He had intended for him all along. God's plan was to use this man's strength in an amazing way.

You may relate to this story and feel like you are pushing a rock. I have certainly been there. The rock is not the focus; you are. What is God showing you to do today? Are you doing it the very best you can?

As you follow and push the rock, you are becoming more like Jesus, stronger in every way, and more ready to help change the world.

Bible Verse:

James 1:2-4 (NIV) – "Consider it pure joy, my brothers and sisters, whenever you face trials of many kinds because you know that the testing of your faith produces perseverance. Let perseverance finish its work so that you may be mature and complete, not lacking anything."

Prayer:

"Dear Jesus, you are my all. I trust in you, even when times are tough. I know that you said there will be challenges in this world but not to worry because you have overcome this world. Help me to remain true to you every day. Please strengthen me, guide me, and direct me. I love you. Please bring your peace that passes all understanding into my heart and soul. I will be who you made me to be. Help me also to love and support those around me who are struggling. In Jesus' name, Amen."

Take Action:

1. List the struggles you are facing now, and note whether each struggle is within or outside of your control.
2. Consider and answer this question: How can you work on the struggles within your control and trust in God for those out of your control?

Additional Resources:

Book - *Unbroken* by Laura Hillenbrand

Movie – *War Room* by the Kendrick Brothers

Music – "Shoulders" by For King and Country

Tool - Perseverance Worksheet at www. madetochangetheworld.com / resources

CHAPTER 10
LIVE YOUR PURPOSE

C hapter Focus: *I hope the first nine chapters of this book got you thinking, and even more importantly, got you moving and growing. The full purpose of this book is to help you to actually live out your purpose--the one that God made you for--each day of your life. This final chapter is about how to do that long-term. It is easy to have a short-term stint of success in nearly anything you do. For example, you could stay on a diet for a few weeks and lose weight, control your spending for a month and save a little bit, or love people really well for a couple of days. However, that is not living out a life change but simply hitting a short term goal. This chapter will cover key elements of long-term change such as sustaining energy, changing habits, and keeping your commitments. Your life and your impact depend upon how you live day by day from here on out.*

HAVING IT ALL

What most people dream of and hope for, Kate Spade had. Most women and men around the world knew her name and her quality purses. According to the world's standards, she had it all. Her estimated net worth was $150,000,000. She had fame, fortune, and all the things everyone would like to have. In June of 2018, she took her own life.

Fame and popularity did not save her, and in fact, made her miserable. She had what many of us dream of, yet in the end, it did not bring happiness. In and of themselves, possessions are not bad, but unfortunately we end up chasing things that in the end still leave us empty. What are you chasing in life?

You can decide to live a life based on your own moods, perceptions, and desires. This may get you temporary satisfaction, but in the end will make you miserable. Don't try to get through life by focusing on things that you will leave behind on this earth. Instead, be a God chaser.

Think about this quote by Philip James Elliot, who died in 1956 while trying to evangelize a remote group of people in Ecuador. He said, "He is no fool who gives what he cannot keep to gain that which he cannot lose." Ultimately, Jim and four others gave their lives trying to minister to this group. However, the wives and families went back and continued this mission, and they completely changed that tribe of people who have been eternally thankful and blessed. If you could ask Jim if the giving of his life was worth it, I am quite confident he would not hesitate to say "Yes". By the way, if you want to see this story in movie form, rent *End of the Spear*, produced in 2005.

THE PARABLE OF THE MEXICAN FISHERMAN

Here is an adaptation of a short story, or parable, originally written by German Author Heinrich Böll. This story teaches many many lessons, including the importance of contentment with what you have and spending time with those God has placed around you.

An American investment banker was taking a much-needed vacation in a small coastal Mexican village when a small boat with just one fisherman docked. The boat held several large, fresh fish.

The investment banker was impressed by the quality of the fish and asked the Mexican how long it took to catch them.

The Mexican replied, "Only a little while."

The banker then asked why he didn't stay out longer and catch more fish?

The Mexican fisherman replied he had enough to support his family's immediate needs.

The American then asked, "But what do you do with the rest of your time?"

The Mexican fisherman replied, "I sleep late, fish a little, play with my children, take a siesta with my wife, and stroll into the village each evening where I sip wine and play my guitar with my amigos; I have a full and busy life, señor."

The investment banker scoffed, "I am an Ivy League MBA, and I could help you. You could spend more time fishing and with the proceeds buy a bigger boat, and with the proceeds from the bigger boat, you could buy several boats until eventually you would have a whole fleet of fishing boats. Instead of selling your catch to the middleman, you could sell directly to the processor, eventually opening your own cannery. You could control the product, processing, and distribution."

Then he added, "Of course, you would need to leave this small coastal fishing village and move to Mexico City where you would run your growing enterprise."

The Mexican fisherman asked, "But señor, how long will this all take?"

To which the American replied, "Fifteen to twenty years."

"But what then?" asked the Mexican.

The American laughed and said, "That's the best part. When the time is right, you would announce an IPO and sell your company stock to the public and become very rich. You could make millions."

"Millions, señor? Then what?"

To which the investment banker replied, "Then you would retire. You could move to a small coastal fishing village where you would sleep late, fish a little, play with your kids, take siestas with your wife, and stroll to the village in the evenings where you could sip wine and play your guitar with your amigos."

The moral of this story is to live life each day and not just focus solely on the American dream. You could work yourself to the bone for 20-30 years and neglect other important areas of life, possibly losing everything. Live life now, on purpose, in peace and by faith. Follow Jesus every day and as my Father-in-Law Luis says, "Enjoy the ride". God will take you on an amazing adventure that will not only change your life but change the lives of those in the world around you.

SHOOTING HOOPS

God put an analogy in my mind many years ago about how we grow in life when we walk with Him. Picture teaching a four or five-year-old child how to shoot a basketball. You would probably start with a little nerf hoop that is four or five feet tall. You might also start with the granny shot. This is executed by using both hands on the ball, lowering it down between your legs, then with both hands hoisting it up into the air.

You show the child this shot, and for the first few days, he is throwing it everywhere. It may not even hit the backboard. But after a while, the kid starts to get it. The ball starts going in once in a while. Then it goes in more often. A week later the child hits most shots and you offer compliments like, "That is perfect!" and "Way to go!" In actuality, compared to the NBA, those shots are nowhere near perfect. They are made on a short hoop, with a nerf ball, and executed granny style. Those shots will definitely not earn him a scholarship, yet for this little boy they are perfect based on his skill and size.

Next, you raise the hoop one foot. Now, most shots are off the mark. What was once perfect has become a constant miss. After a few more days of practice, your little understudy really starts to get it and gets more consistent with the six-foot hoop. Again, you offer encouraging comments about how perfect the shots are. Then you REALLY change it up by demonstrating the overhand shot. Now the young player is missing everything. Yesterday he felt like the king of the world and today--a big loser. Shots are missing the hoop and even the backboard. Nothing is going in.

You keep encouraging the young child not to give up. You model the shot in more detail. After a few weeks he gets pretty good at it, with a form that is really starting to look like a basketball player and soon again you are saying, "Perfect job!" Over the months and years, you keep raising the hoop, switching balls, and fine-tuning the shot until one day, your student is flawless in technique.

This is the way we grow in our Christian faith. Wherever you are right now in your faith and walk with God, He wants to help you "perfect" that spot. It does not mean you will be perfect like Jesus, but you will be constantly moving into a place more and more like Him as your faith grows. Don't stop working on your "shot". If you give up, you will never grow. Your spiritual "shot" is spending daily time with God, memorizing and living His Word, believing by faith and not sight, and when times get really tough, crying out for God to save you.

It can be frustrating at times. Keep your focus and work on your foundation, and you will perfect it. It may take time and cause you to change and grow in ways you can never imagine. Stand confident in God's promises. He will raise you up to be more like Him on this earth until one day you go to be with Him in heaven. Persevere and trust all the way.

THE SOURCE OF YOUR ENERGY

In order to do as Paul says in the Bible--which is to approach our lives like a marathon, not a sprint, with God--we need to have some key factors in place, such as energy and positive habits. Let's start with how to have the energy you need to finish the race God has for you each and every day.

As you may guess, human energy comes from the source of all energy of this world: God. Genesis 2:7 (ASV) gives an account of how God made the first man: "And Jehovah God formed man of the dust of the ground, and breathed into his nostrils the breath of life, and man became a living soul." The term "breath of life" is also translated as

"Spirit". So God breathed His Spirit into a form that He made from the earth's dirt and the first human came to life.

There was no life or energy in our bodies until God, the energy of life and life-giver, put it into us. He is the very spark of life and still to this very day sustains all human life. Even in today's day and age, modern scientists can duplicate a human body but they cannot bring it to life. Only God is the life-giver and energy force within us.

Here is what modern science has found. In the *Made to Change the World* coach training materials there is a section about neurons, which says:

"The flow of electrical energy in the human body takes place in what are called neurons. There are 10 billion neurons throughout the human body that allow electrical impulses to flow from the brain to every part of the body. These neurons, which are made of physical and electrical components, impulse from one to another and allow you to walk, talk, move, make decisions, and literally live. Your brain -- which is your heart, soul and mind-- is that 'electrical switch' that allows you to think, do, and be."

Modern science can duplicate chemical components that make up a human body, but not the electrical components. In other words, humans can physically put together a body, but they cannot bring it to life. This is because the energy source of who we are, the breath of God (spirit), is the only life-giving force.

Here is my personal belief from my understanding of the Bible and a limited understanding of biology and science. I believe our energy is from God and cannot be duplicated. I also believe this energy exists in our spirit and in our neurons and that it travels through our brain and body. It causes us to be able to think, move, talk, keep our bodily functions going, etc.

Along this same line of thought, the fullness of energy for our human bodies comes from the balance of the chemical and electrical components. For example, what we do to impact the electrical (or spirit) part of our being includes things like meditation (for Christians, that means prayer and dwelling upon God), learning, sleeping, avoiding high stress, and exercise, to name a few. The things that impact the chemical part of our body directly are what we eat and drink, outside toxins that come in, etc. This points to the way drugs and excessive alcohol impact our body's balance and functioning. Proper balance in each component is important for optimal health. Imagine how out of balance you can become through addictions and poor life choices.

HOW TO INCREASE YOUR ENERGY

Although some of the following may sound like worldly knowledge, I believe there are elements of science that prove how God has made us and validates what gives us energy in this life to do the things we are designed to do. Science simply tries to explain what God has created.

Keeping up the "electrical" energy requires that we do the things that increase it and avoid the things that decrease it. Here is a list of areas to rank for yourself:

Answer how you typically do in these areas that impact "electrical" energy:

1. Spend a relaxed time with God (meditating on Him, prayer, scripture) daily
2. Get enough sleep each night for your body and mind to recover
3. Exercise and move your body (as we were designed to do from Genesis)
4. Learn something new to stretch your mind
5. Read motivating and uplifting material
6. Focus on the Purpose, Mission, and Vision God has given you
7. Have God-directed goals you are working towards
8. Focus on God and don't give in to fear
9. Correct any mental "addictions" such as pornography, lying, cheating, etc.
10. Give gratitude to God and others

Answer how you typically do in these areas that impact your "chemical" balance":

1. Put healthy foods into your body
2. Eat the right amount of food for your body
3. Generally avoid unhealthy foods (sugar, alcohol, chemically altered foods, etc.)
4. Avoid drug-related chemicals (except as prescribed by Doctors)
5. Correct any chemical "addictions" to food, smoking, alcohol, drugs, etc.

MOMENTUM

Famed US Women's Soccer star Mia Hamm stated that "Success breeds success". This is very true and powerful. What this really means is that when we as humans find that we have gotten something "right" or accomplished, it encourages us to know we can be successful at the next thing. This is especially true when it comes to faith in God. When we do even the smallest of things, such as starting each day by reading a verse and having a short prayer, it can then lead to more time with God and a closer relationship with Him.

When we take a small step of faith, such as inviting someone to church, whether or not they come, it motivates us to do it while trusting that God is working through us. The reverse is also true. As physics 101 points out, an object at rest stays at rest and an object in motion stays in motion; it is important to understand what starts and stops motion.

In our lives, most people want to change something, especially when it comes to walking with God. What, then, actually gets us to act on it? The answer is a combination of emotions, logic, and will, as discussed in Lesson 7. Zig Ziglar used to say that people are changed by inspiration or desperation. We have to become emotionally and willfully charged enough that the fear of staying the same is greater than the fear of change, or--even more powerfully stated--the vision of, and desire for, a better outcome outweighs the fear of change.

Here are two true-life examples:

1. I once coached a pastor who had just been released from the hospital after major heart surgery. The doctor told him he needed to make major health changes soon or he wouldn't be long for this life. He did. Without that "push", he probably wouldn't have prioritized this changed behavior for his life.
2. I once coached a husband and wife who were starting a business, and the vision of helping others through medical billing and having more financial freedom to do more for God propelled them to form a company and move forward.

A study was conducted several decades ago about motivation, and the results were combined into what is now called the Self Determination Theory by Edward Deci and Richard Ryan. The theory states that there are three key areas that help someone become and stay motivated. They are:

1. Autonomy - Where the person feels they have choices in the situation and are not forced to do something. From a spiritual perspective, God gives each of us autonomy which may also be called "free will".
2. Competence - This is self-efficacy and means the person has some success, maybe even in other areas of life, upon which to draw to achieve success again. This again means that momentum fuels momentum. Our faith in God also works similarly.
3. Relatedness - This means having someone or a group of others to support the person, which is such a critical value given by a coach. Coaches should also help others find additional support in life, such as mentors, small groups, pastors, etc.

Even the smallest success recognized by a person can give the belief, confidence, and energy to work towards additional success. In coaching, it is always important to search for and then recognize the minutest success a person has achieved. In our Christian lives, it is even more important to recognize what God has done for you or how He is present in the process with you through current struggle and changes. Such recognition builds your faith in God.

HABITS

John Maxwell, leader of leaders, had this to say about habits: "You'll never change your life until you change something you do daily. The secret of your success is found in your daily routine." To go along with this, Sean Covey said, "Depending on what they are, our habits will either make us or break us. We become what we repeatedly do."

The Merriam Webster Dictionary defines the word habit as follows:

1) a settled tendency or usual manner of behavior,

2) an acquired mode of behavior that has become nearly or completely involuntary,

3) a behavior pattern acquired by frequent repetition or physiologic exposure that shows itself in regularity or increased facility of performance,

4) the prevailing disposition or character of a person's thoughts and feelings: mental makeup

There are good habits that lead you toward God and your purpose, mission, and vision. These can be such things as keeping a devotional time with God, going to church, praying with your spouse, taking care of your health, planning your finances, etc. There are also bad habits that can easily pull you off track from moving toward God and your goals, such as watching TV for several hours per day, continually procrastinating on important things, and not making time for God or the important people in your life.

To be clear, I am defining habits differently from addictions, which are strong inclinations to do, use, or indulge in something repeatedly. Addictions are compulsive, chronic, physiological, or psychological needs for a habit-forming substance, behavior, or activity having harmful physical, psychological, or social effects and typically causing well-defined symptoms (such as anxiety, irritability, tremors, or nausea) upon withdrawal or abstinence (Merriam Webster Dictionary).

Both habits and addictions are important to deal with in order to really live the life God has for you. In general, working with a partner, coach, or mentor, habits can be identified, planned for, and changed as God enables you to do so. In dealing with addictions, it is important to partner with someone specifically trained in that area, such as a Christian Counselor or Psychologist to provide a deeper focus at a spiritual and emotional level to make these changes. Here is what is most important to know when dealing with habits and addictions: God loves you. He will help you make the changes He is calling you to make. As you partner with Godly people to help you through, your life will change to give you more peace, confidence, and fulfillment.

There are many directives in God's word about our habits and what they should be. Here are some key scriptures to start.

Romans 12:2 ESV "Do not be conformed to this world, but be transformed by the renewal of your mind, that by testing you may discern what is the will of God, what is good and acceptable and perfect."

1 Thessalonians 5:17-18 ESV "Pray without ceasing, give thanks in all circumstances; for this is the will of God in Christ Jesus for you."

Philippians 4:8 ESV "Finally, brothers, whatever is true, whatever is honorable, whatever is just, whatever is pure, whatever is lovely, whatever is commendable, if there is any excellence, if there is anything worthy of praise, think about these things.

1 Corinthians 10:31 ESV "So, whether you eat or drink, or whatever you do, do all to the glory of God."

Most people believe that it takes 21 days to change a habit. Others think it's 40 days. From one study I read years ago, it takes anywhere from 17-256 days to change a habit, depending on the person and the specific thing they are trying to change. As Zig Ziglar said, "If you always do what you've always done, you'll always get what you always got." To put it another way, without working on habits, your life will not change.

Prioritizing the following habits in your life will bring you closer to
God and help you follow the purpose and plan He has for you.

1. Spend time with God every day – Many years ago, I started
   doing this just 10 minutes per day and it changed my life. I
   now spend about an hour each day; it is how I start each day,
   and it is the singular most important part of my day. For some
   simple tips on how to start spending time with God daily, go to
   www.madetochangetheworld.com.

2. Choose to love each person every day – Remember from an
   earlier chapter, love is not an emotion, but a choice. Love is
   also the greatest calling of our lives. When Jesus was asked
   what is the greatest commandment from God, He replied:
   "Love the Lord your God with all your heart, soul, mind, and
   strength". Jesus also gave a bonus answer saying the second
   greatest commandment is to love our neighbors as ourselves
   (Matthew 22:36-40). Review Chapter 2 for all the aspects of
   love and how you can live these out in life.

3. Keep the right attitude in life – We cannot control many things
   in this life, but we can (and are expected to) control our
   attitudes. I cannot put it any better than Chuck Swindoll
   summarized it:

"The longer I live, the more I realize the impact of attitude on life. Attitude, to me, is more important than facts. It is more important than the
past, than education, than money, than circumstances, than failures,
than successes, than what other people think, say or do. It is more
important than appearance, giftedness or skill. It will make or break a
company... a church... a home.

The remarkable thing is we have a choice every day regarding the attitude we embrace for that day. We cannot change our past... we cannot
change the fact that people will act in a certain way. We cannot change
the inevitable. The only thing we can do is play the one string we
have, and that is our attitude...

I am convinced that life is 10% what happens to me and 90% how I react to it.

And so it is with you... we are in charge of our Attitudes"

You may also want to prayerfully consider improving habits in the areas of reviewing your balance wheel (Chapter 5), looking at the areas of self-control (Chapter 8) and learning to persevere with God (Chapter 9). When you seek God for direction, He will not only show you where to make new Godly habits, but will also help you put them into place through the power of His Holy Spirit.

One final tip when it comes to breaking bad habits. There is a phrase I have used continually in coaching, which is that you cannot just get rid of a bad habit--you have to replace it with a good one. It is much more effective to focus on what you want in place and how you want to live than to focus specifically on not doing something. For example, if you want to break the habit of sleeping in so you have time with God, focus on setting the habit of getting up at a specific time vs. trying not to sleep in. This proactive approach will get you the result you desire.

Building new habits can feel like a lot of work and a real struggle at the beginning. The good news is that this is only for a while. If you stick with it, a new habit becomes a new lifestyle. This new self-discipline becomes a new way of living. Over time, you will not need to keep trying to push yourself to love others, have devotions in the morning, or whatever you are trying to change. It will become part of who you are. While your struggle early on had your old habit working against you, your new habit will soon work for you, prompting you to continue doing it.

KEEP GROWING

As you continue to grow in your faith and relationship with God, here are some other important factors that will help you become all He has designed you to become and live on purpose for Him.

1. Continually Surrender. Walking with God is not about how much you can do for Him and prove to others. It is really about what you will turn over to Him and follow. Every day, you should be surren-

dering all that you have and all that you are to Him. When you hold onto things, you begin taking over for God, but when you turn them over, you are letting God be God in your life. What I like to do periodically in my devotional time is lie face down and flat and in my mind think of all the things God has given me and done for me and turn them all back over to Him to use as He wants.

One powerful example of this that hit home in my life many years ago was when Claudia and I were getting ready to move back to California. We had literally everything we owned in a moving truck parked in my parents' driveway that night, and as I was getting ready for bed, I realized that if someone stole the truck, everything we owned would be gone. Everything. And I was OK with that. The most important things in my life are not things. They are people: my Heavenly Father, my wife, my family, and those around me whom God has called me to love.

2. Establish Accountability. When you live as an island unto yourself not letting anyone in, you are bound to stumble and not have any help to get up. Be willing to be close to others. First, be accountable to God. Allow Him into every area of your life so that He may show you, lead you, and guide you. When you fall or when you fail, come to Him. He already knows, but when you humble yourself in accountability, He will lift you up to rise above. When I think of raising Ellie, I recall that she came onto this earth without knowing anything and needing to learn everything as she grows. As I help her learn and grow step by step, I grow closer to her and it brings me joy. That is how your Heavenly Father wants to be with you.

Also, be accountable to others. My wife and I are very close. I am accountable to her on all levels, and she to me. We grow together in this way. I am also accountable to my brother-in-law, Jonathan. Every week, we pray together, talk about our balance with each other, confess our shortfalls, and support each other. I also have accountability through coaching for following the Purpose, Mission, and Vision for which God has me on this earth, which helps me stay on God's track. Who in your life is keeping you accountable?

3. Know that you know. I will never forget the words spoken directly to me by my mentor Zig Ziglar. After spending 45 minutes with him one day backstage at a large event in Cleveland, Ohio, Zig looked me in the eye and said, "Brian, I know that I know that I know that I am doing exactly what God has called me to do and I will continue to do so until I leave this earth." It gave me chills! How can you absolutely know you are doing what God has called you to do? That is what I wanted and what I believe I am doing today.

You can absolutely know God and know that you are being and doing what He wants you to do. In the Bible, God says "You will seek me and find me when you seek me with all your heart" Jeremiah 29:13 (NIV). If your focus is to seek God not only will you find Him, but He will lead you day by day and step by step. As I mentioned before, my purpose for each day is to believe as I go to lay my head on my pillow that God says to me "Well done good and faithful servant" Matthew 25:23 (NIV). If you strive to know God, hear God and follow Him everything else in your life will come together through Him and you will be a world changer.

PUT IT ALL TOGETHER

Let's put all of this together. You have just read a book about how God has made you to change the world. Maybe you laughed at some stories and cried at others. Hopefully, you learned some new things and felt inspired along the way. Ideally, you found something you can take away from this book.

I want to challenge you now to realize that it doesn't really matter if you liked the book or didn't like it, if you learned something new or not, if you were moved by a story or two or didn't feel a thing. What really matters most is how you will act upon what you read. Learning is one thing and doing is quite another. It's just like faith: you can say you have faith or you can live out your faith.

Let's reflect upon the chapters of this book. I want you to note "yes" or "no" based on each chapter to answer if you are actually doing it or not. The chapters are listed as building blocks, so wherever you write your first "no" is the place for you to start. That may mean you will need to re-read that chapter. Think about it and pray about it. Determine how and when you will act upon it.

Chapter 1 – Do you have a perspective of life like Jerome, that your life matters?

Chapter 2 – Have you written out your life purpose and committed to living it?

Chapter 3 – Are you putting only truth in your mind and turning away from all else?

Chapter 4 – Are you sure of what you hope for and certain of what you do not see?

Chapter 5 – Are you acting upon your faith and not just saying you have faith?

Chapter 6 – Do you exert self-control in the areas that God asks you to?

Chapter 7 – Is your life in balance with Jesus as the central hub?

Chapter 8 – Are you persevering and learning what God wants you to right now?

Chapter 9 – Do you have a plan for letting God direct your steps?

Chapter 10 - Are you fully living your purpose today?

For more ideas on how to change the world in your daily life, be sure to read the following epilogue. We have also developed helpful tools at Made to Change the World to actually help you apply what you learn-- not just to store information in your brain, but to live it! Go to www. madetochangetheworld.com and look for resources, coaching, tools, emails, small group study, etc.

Bible Verse:

1 Peter 1:16 (NKJV) – "Be holy, for I am holy."

Prayer:

"Dear Lord Jesus, you are my everything. I want to be holy as you are holy. Please cleanse me and lead me every day. Help me know that I know that I know your voice and that I am being and doing exactly what you want me to be and do each day until the day I go to be with you. I live to love you and others. Help me to live life with the goal of hearing "Well done, good and faithful servant" at the end of each day. In Jesus' name, Amen."

Take Action:

1. Make a list of everything that's yours in this life, then write "surrendered" next to each.
2. Ask God at the end of each day if He would say "Well done" and journal what He says.

Additional Resources:

Book – *Over the Top* by Zig Ziglar

Movie – *End of the Spear* Produced by Every Tribe Entertainment

Music – "My Desire" by Jeremy Camp

Tool - *Made to Change the World Small Group Study* www.madetochangetheworld.com

EPILOGUE

WHAT IS NEXT?

Focus: *Now that you have read through this book, you may have different thoughts or emotions. This book may inspire you to want to do something different in your life. Made to Change the World could challenge your thinking or even frustrate you at times. The goal of this book is to cause you to really decide what you believe, look for truth, then base your life on it. God has a big plan for you, but it is not just one to consider, but one to live out. We only have one life to live. The best life to live is the one that was originally designed in the Garden of Eden where we walk closely with God, love Him, learn from Him, and live out our purpose on this earth. The huge bonus to doing all of this is that it only gets better once we leave this world and go to heaven. Here are some ways to live full out for God and help change the world while doing so.*

LIVE IT OUT

Reading a book is one thing. Living it out is quite another. I am not referring to this book, but the Bible. This book was written to cause you to take a good look at your life now, to determine in your own mind if you believe there is a God and who you think He is. Then it challenges you to decide if you will live your life completely based on what you believe. This book was not written to try and force anyone to believe in Jesus. It was written in love and with hope that you would consider that there is a God who truly loves you, wants to walk with you, and has an amazing plan for your life. The choice is up to you to decide if you want to believe it and if you want to base your life on it.

My wife and I had the fortunate opportunity to travel to Italy some years ago. We were able to see the famous David statue. It is almost surreal to see this massive stone that has incredible detail and was made into a masterpiece. At one point Michael was asked how he made this incredible work of art and he said that he chipped away everything that wasn't David. Michael could see the masterpiece within the stone. God sees the masterpiece in you. It does not matter what your past was. It does not matter the things you have done, If you will let him chip away things in your life that are not you, the result will be the true you, His greatest creation.

The amazing thing about God is that He doesn't just chip away at your life to remove all the sin, filth, and pain to make you like new. He does not force His way. He waits, and He knocks at the door of your heart. He calls out to you. If you don't want to listen or change, you do not have to. The choice is up to you. However, if you decide to turn everything over to God, your walk with Him is a process. It then requires you to make changes as He leads you to. Some changes are not difficult. Other changes will challenge the very core of things you have believed or stored in your heart for a long time.

As a reminder from an earlier chapter, the first step to change is awareness. God will make you aware of new things as you follow Him. Things to change. Things to do. Things to create. As you get this awareness from God, do not be afraid. If God calls you to do something, He will give you the strength and wisdom to carry it out. The key to walking with God is knowing that He is with you always and living based on that truth. Joshua 1:9 says, "Have I not commanded you? Be strong and courageous. Do not be afraid; do not be discouraged, for the Lord your God will be with you wherever you go."

LITTLE THINGS CAN HAVE A HUGE IMPACT

In the world today, sports figures are some of our biggest heroes. Unfortunately, many are poor role models. Some athletes could have a positive impact on this world but unfortunately have the opposite impact. Although on the court or field they are very talented, without God they are no stronger than anyone else against this world's temptations and struggles. It is hard to be in this world and follow God. It is harder still to be in the limelight and on the world stage and not only live for God but speak it publicly. Thankfully, there are men and women who have stepped up to do this.

TWO MEN OF RECENT TIMES WHO STAND OUT ARE TIM TEBOW AND STEPH Curry. Tim Tebow, currently playing professional baseball, was a national hero at a young age in college football. As the quarterback of the Florida Gators from 2006 to 2009, he set many records including being the first sophomore to win the Heisman trophy and winning the College Football National Championship as a Junior. Tim never held back about sharing his faith in Jesus, and still does to this day. He was known for putting Bible scriptures in his eye black (a grease or strip applied under the eye to reduce glare) for his games. In the 2009 BCS Championship game, he wrote "John 3:16" and that small action caused more than 90 million Google searches in 24 hours for that one verse. Sure, Tim already had a large audience, but he was not afraid to do the seemingly small things that could help change the world.

Wardell Stephen Curry II, better known as Steph Curry, is another example of standing up to share his faith. An NBA basketball Golden State Warrior, he has accomplished amazing things. Named the most valuable player twice, he won the NBA championship with his team three times and has been called the greatest shooter of all time. He is even credited with revolutionizing the game by inspiring a greater use of the three-point shot. With all that he has accomplished on the court, he continues to talk about the most important thing to him, which is his relationship with Jesus Christ. One example is in an MVP speech in which he stated, "People should know who I represent and why I am who I am, and it's all because of my Lord and Savior." One thing for which he is most noted is his basketball shoelace scripted with "4:13", a reference to the Bible verse Philippians 4:13, which reads: "I can do all things through Christ who strengthens me." Again, while this seems like a small thing, it continually witnesses to others.

Few people have the world spotlight like these athletes, yet we can all do little things that people notice. Think of how you can have an impact for God on those around you. It could be in what you say, what you do, or even something that starts a conversation about your faith. Remember, God has you in the right section with the right people to be the best witness for Him.

WHAT TO DO NEXT

We are all conditioned in this day and age to find the secret step, to get the sequence to success. Tell me A, B, and C of what I need to do to get the result. That is not how God works. Sometimes what you think should be step 10 is step 2 and vice versa. What I am not going to do in the book is say this is exactly what you should do, except for the very first recommendation. That is the most important. All the others may change as led by God or in sequence as led by God.

Recommendation 1 – Start spending time with God every day. Even if it is 5 minutes. During this time, read something in the Bible and pray. For additional resources on this, go to www. madetochangetheworld.com.

Recommendation 2 – Find a Bible believing church. Ideally, you go to the church and not just attend online but if you are stuck in a place where you cannot get out, then virtual is an option. Find a place that is loving but imperfect, because none will be perfect.

Recommendation 3 – Take the steps that are written in this book. In Chapter 10, there are suggestions about going back through the book in key areas that stood out to you or are sticking points.

Recommendation 4 – Sign up for the free weekly emails on the Made to Change the World website. You will receive videos, questions to help you go deeper, and other tools to help you walk closer with God.

Recommendation 5 – Start or join a small group. It is important to be around other believers who also struggle daily to surrender to God and grow together.

Recommendation 6 – Every week for at least six months, complete the Surrender Wheel. You will see how you are growing with God and where to focus. Also, keep track of your goals and review them weekly as well.

Recommendation 7 – Have someone that helps you walk closer with Jesus. Have someone in your life whom you trust with your life and who walks with God, and meet consistently. You can check out CTW Coaching on our website for support.

Recommendation 8 – Determine how you will use your time, talents, and/or resources in some way to help change the world. The little things you do are not little--they are life-changing and God notices. Remember the starfish story!

Here are some ideas God may use to spur you into actions to change the world. As you do anything with your time, talent, and treasures, be someone who is willing to share the love of Jesus through prayer, encouragement, and personal witness.

Time:

- Volunteer at church
- Volunteer to feed the hungry
- Volunteer to help orphans
- Visit people who are lonely
- Visit the elderly
- Invite someone to pray with you
- Start a small group
- Become a foster parent
- Adopt a child
- Sign up for a prayer ministry
- Coordinate a block party, then pray before dinner
- Invite neighbors to church
- Go on a mission trip

- Call the person who offended you and make peace
- Spend an hour per day with your children
- Eat with your family and ask them what God has done in their lives
- Do something unexpected for a neighbor
- Ask your closest friend if s/he has ever accepted Jesus
- Ask your family members if they have ever accepted Jesus
- Tell those around you that you love and care for them

Talent:

- Make a meal for someone
- Draw a picture for someone
- Sing
- Create something new
- Write a book
- Lead a church group
- Teach kids or adults about Jesus
- Plan a day trip to be with your family
- Help someone with their finances
- Smile and make conversation with others
- Get into ministry
- Encourage someone who is down
- Help others find and use their talents
- Become a Coach
- Play on a sports team
- Help someone organize their house

Treasures:

- Tithe 10% of your income to church
- Give to ministries
- Give to others around you in need
- Give away unused clothes
- Give away unused toys

- Buy Christian books for others (I can think of a really good one)
- Share your home
- Give to the poor
- Feed the homeless
- Donate a car to a family in need
- Give airline tickets or miles to someone in need
- Give away winter wear to those who are cold
- Pay someone's toll road ticket
- Pay someone's utility bill
- Ask your pastor what is needed for the church
- Support someone going on a mission trip

As you can tell, there are many ways to begin changing the world. Pray to see what God puts on your heart. Don't wait to start changing the world around you. There are people who need you and need to see God through you today.

This is your time! Act on your faith. Follow as God leads. Change as He calls you to chip away to reveal the masterpiece. Love others today with your time, talent, and treasures. Do not wait, as there is a lost and dying world around you that needs to see God in you.

FINAL LYRICS

I thought for now I would leave you with these lyrics from the song *That's How You Change the World* by the Newsboys.

That's how you change the world

That's how you change the world

ALL MY LIFE I HAD BIG DREAMS

To do big things and make a change

And all the while I just passed by the simple needs

Right here next to me

Cause there's a breaking heart

That's falling apart and tear-filled eyes

Looking back at me

God, won't you help me to see

It's a prayer in an empty room

Little things we do when nobody's around

A hand reaching out

To a heart in doubt

It's the smallest spark

That can light the dark

That's how you change the world

That's how you change the world

A million little drops of rain

Can be enough to cause a tidal wave

A flood of your love that no one can contain

'Cause there's an empty soul that wants to be known

Around me now that I can lead to you

Revealing love that won't refuse

It's the kind words

A simple smile

More than showing up

Going the extra mile

It's giving everything

When you've got nothing left

Sharing a little hope

With a single breath

That's how you change the world

That's how you change the world

FINAL THOUGHTS

Although I have written this book, I always must stay tuned into God
to know how He wants to use me for His kingdom. My wife and I stay
very involved in volunteering at church, as well as giving our tithes
and additional amounts to places like American Bible Society and
Compassion International. I work hard both at work and outside of
work to try and stay on God's schedule and always make it my
priority to have meals and time with my family each day. There are
times, however, when I forget to check on my elderly neighbors whose
health is failing. I always desire to call previous friends and family
from across the country to encourage and pray for them, and sometimes I miss it.

None of us is perfect, nor will we be until we get to heaven. What God
desires for us is to live our daily life as best we can to glorify Him
while always being tuned in to the ways we can love others around us
even though it may not have been planned in our schedule or
checkbook.

In Matthew 25, Jesus tells the parable about a rich man who entrusted
three of his servants to take care of his wealth while he was gone. One
servant buried the treasure (which for us can mean our time, talents,
and resources) and his master was very unhappy with him. The master
even took away the money and gave it to another, more faithful,
servant. The second servant invested the money and had seen it multi-
ply. The third servant had done the same and saw even more prosper-
ity. Matthew 25:23 says, "His master replied, 'Well done good and
faithful servant. You have been faithful with a few things; I will put

you in charge of many things. Come and share your master's happiness.'"

I have come to realize that this parable expresses how each of us should strive to live our daily lives for God. We should be faithful to know our master, to understand His will, and to follow as He calls. I believe the greatest thing at the end of each day and at the end of my life for God to say, "I love you, my son. You have been faithful to me in all the areas of your life. Well done. Come and share in my happiness." Imagine God saying that to you right now, at the end of each day, and after your last day on earth. I hope and pray that the *Made to Change the World* book, small group study, and other resources will help you do just that. May God bless you today and every day. I hope to meet you one day, whether on this earth or for eternity in heaven.

CONGRATULATIONS ON COMPLETING

MADE TO CHANGE THE WORLD

By Coach Brian Williams

Live your life as a World Changer for Christ!

To remind you that you are changing the world, I have made a completion certificate for you. Please post your review of this book on Amazon, then click this link to get your completion certificate. www.madetochangetheworld.com/certificate

You can collect all MTCTW certificates by completing:

1) Made to Change the World book

2) Made to Change the World Small Group Study

3) Made to Change the World Small Group Leader

4) Made to Change the World Monthly Member

5) Made to Change the World Coach Training

6) Made to Change the World Pastor / Ministry Leader

APPENDIX A

LIST OF SCRIPTURES TO STAND ON

Romans 8

Proverbs 3

Jeremiah 29:11-14

Psalm 45:1-7

Psalm 28:1-2

Joshua 1:9-10 -

Psalm 50:9-15

Isaiah 26:3

Ephesians 6:10-18

Philippians 3:12-14

Philippians 4:4-8

Philippians 4:12-13

Proverbs 17:27-28

Psalm 19:12-13

1 Chronicles 4:9-10

Ephesians 5:23-28

John 3:16

James 1:19-20

James 1:22

Colossians 3:23-24

Colossians 3:5-6

1 Timothy 5:1-2

Galatians 5:22-23

1 Corinthians 13:3-7

Isaiah 44:2

Romans 6:13

2 Timothy 4:5

1 John 3:16

Proverbs 10:22

Ephesians 3:20

2 Corinthians 9:8

Titus 2:11-12

Nehemiah 4:14

1 Samuel 2:8

2 Chronicles 7:14

John 1:12

Psalm 119:9-11

John 16:24

Matthew 21:22

1 John 5:14-15

Acts 1:8

1 Peter 3:15

1 Corinthians 10:13

Joshua 1:8

Psalm 95:6-7

Psalm 113:9

Psalm 116

Proverbs 25:28

Psalm 121:1-3

Ecclesiastes 5:19-20

Galatians 6:9

Jeremiah 17:10

1 John 2:5-6

Galatians 5:16-17

Isaiah 30:15

Isaiah 29:16

Ezekiel 36:26

James 3:13

Colossians 1:28

Hebrews 12:11

Acts 4:13

Lamentations 3:22-23

John 14:27

2 Corinthians 12:9-11

Acts 20:24